C-SCAPE

C-SCAPE

Conquer the Forces

Changing Business Today

L A R R Y   K R A M E R

HARPER
BUSINESS

An Imprint of HarperCollins*Publishers*
www.harpercollins.com

FIRST EDITION

Designed by Eric Butler

Library of Congress Cataloging-in-Publication Data

Kramer, Larry, 1950–
    C-scape : conquer the forces changing business today / Larry Kramer.
    p.   cm.
    ISBN 978-0-06-198497-6
    1. Customer services. 2. Marketing. 3. Advertising. I. Title.
HF5415.5.K68   2010
658.8—dc22

                                                        2010024433

10 11 12 13 14 OV/RRD 10 9 8 7 6 5 4 3 2 1

AUTHOR'S NOTE

I am indebted to my colleague G. F. Lichtenberg for his invaluable assistance. He is a wonderful researcher and writer, a ferocious organizer, and a terrific alter ego. Time after time he was able to see patterns emerge from my two years of research and reporting, sometimes sooner than I did. He helped me immensely by challenging my conclusions, forcing me to dig deeper and deeper for evidence. I could not have written this book without him.

CONTENTS

INTRODUCTION: *Every Business Is a Media Business*   1

► **PART ONE   THE C-SCAPE: HOW DID WE GET HERE?**

The Four Factors Shaping the C-Scape   19

1 *The First Factor: Consumers Choose*   23

2 *The Second Factor: Content Becomes King*   35

3 *The Third Factor: Curation Cures Information Overload*   43

4 *The Fourth Factor: Convergence Remakes Communication—and Organizations*   57

► **PART TWO   WHAT HAPPENS TO MARKETS?**

5 *Marketing beyond the Purchase Funnel*   69

6 *Talk With, Not At*   91

7 *Digital Mindreading*   109

► **PART THREE   WHAT HAPPENS TO PRODUCTS?**

8 *Is Everything "Content"?*   125

9 *They Choose, but You Curate*   135

10 *Loyalty That Lasts*   153

► PART FOUR **WHAT HAPPENS TO BUSINESSES?**

11 *Price the Experience, Not the Product* **167**
12 *Partner Like a Start-up* **183**
13 *The New Newsroom* **207**

ACKNOWLEDGMENTS **225**
INDEX **231**

C-SCAPE

EVERY BUSINESS IS A MEDIA BUSINESS

It was 2007, and Jon Raj, then head of digital marketing for Visa, saw an opportunity. The Internet was maturing as a place for commerce, and small businesses were finding new ways to use it. Competition for Visa's small-business clients was growing. Raj saw the chance to meet the marketing challenges of this increasingly demanding environment not by refining the Visa message, but by doing more for Visa clients than the company had attempted before.

Until then, Visa Business had positioned itself as the company that understood its clients' situations. In addition to print and television advertisements promoting that message, it also offered a website called Your Business, with videos of client success stories. But Raj wanted to go beyond promising to understand clients' needs and celebrating their successes. He wanted to prove to clients that Visa understood them by providing practical help with their most pressing business concerns.

Small-business clients were increasingly caught up in day-to-day problem solving. As Raj explains, "Small business owners want to focus on what they love to do. A designer doesn't get into design to do taxes, handle legal issues," or master Internet marketing and sales. The obligations of the small-business owner could become overwhelming, especially as the speed and technological complexity of business increased.

Visa identified a still-new online platform, created and mainly used by college students, called Facebook. The company took the chance that it might also serve as a place for small businesses to find the partners and advisors they needed to make their companies run more smoothly. On Facebook it created the Visa Business Network or VBN—a "back office" for small-business owners where they could connect with other businesses and customers. Visa partnered with the *Wall Street Journal* to create an "Ask the Experts" feature on the page, and arranged for leading small-business experts from *Entrepreneur* to participate in question-and-answer forums and to write expert advice columns. Other media and business partners provided exclusive small-business news feeds, videos, blogs, and editorial commentary about issues such as cash-flow management, new ways to attract customers, and cost management. In addition, Visa offered the first 20,000 businesses that joined VBN a $100 Facebook Ads credit, to help them learn to use the site to target the precise audiences they needed to reach.

In a sense, the digital marketing department was reinventing the entire business model. Raj sees this as part of a larger transformation. "When marketers create fan pages or communication with prospects and customers," Raj explains, "they're no longer just advertisers . . . they are publishers of content. When they create an app or widget, they are software companies. And when they listen to what customers and critics are saying back to them, they are public relations, customer service and even product development."

What had seemed like a straightforward marketing decision led Visa Business to change not just *how* it sold its products and service, but *what* it sold—and even how a part of the company was understood and organized.

Across business, we are all discovering that the world in which we work and live is transforming faster and more profoundly than ever. Everyone knows that. What's not well understood is that every aspect of these changes—from the transformed landscape of business to the specific challenges that Visa and other businesses are facing to the solutions to those problems—all have the same source: changes in media.

Why media? Because every aspect of business is increasingly carried out through media. From advertising and marketing to sales and customer service, from product design and development to recruitment and employee relations, from the factory floor to shareholder meetings, everything that happens in business is ever more likely to happen on a screen or a handheld device. Business is conducted through what we call "media"—but media, at least media as we've known it until recently, is in serious trouble.

TECHNOLOGY IS ONLY THE BEGINNING

I advise companies around the world and in a range of industries, and everywhere I go, there is no hotter topic than the future of media itself—and none, I think, more wrongly understood. Traditional media is in a death spiral, yet if you ask anyone to explain the ongoing wreck, you will likely hear the same reply, which is correct, familiar, and largely useless. Why are the great metropolitan newspapers, once the profitable pillars of democracy, hemorrhaging billions and struggling to survive? Why are the business models that made possible generations of blockbusters in music, publishing, and television now collapsing? Why are media businesses of all kinds being forced to reinvent themselves?

The common answer is "new technology." From personal computers to the Internet to smartphones to the tablet, there's a familiar list of fairly recent innovations whose widespread adoption has made once-separate forms of media—text, image, audio, and video—available together in one place. This "technological convergence" of multiple forms onto single devices and online platforms sent traditional media into its decline, while it put astonishing new powers in the hands of individuals, changing life for every business that depends on communication—that is, for every business, and for all of us.

Isn't that explanation correct? Yes. But it's not much help on a practical level. It doesn't tell us how to face the challenges of this transitional era in which every means of sharing information is changing. Every kind of storytelling, from news stories to family news, from mass entertainment to literature—including every tool we use to describe a product or a shape a relationship between business and customer—is under pressure to evolve. Organizations and individuals alike feel pressed to set up "broadcast operations" to share their news and information. We move through an ever-growing maze of devices, social networks, and hybrid media forms, and our success depends on how we understand and adapt to this new reality of endlessly flowing information and stories. Whether our goal is a new job or a closer connection to ever-busier family and friends, a rehabilitation of a discredited brand or a successful product launch, we must choose among a growing list of still-evolving media options—too many choices, it often seems, with too few hours in the day. We may not all work in media, but we all live in it.

Even among the new-technology enthusiasts, few know how to

think profitably about the deeper factors shaping our future. We must do more than observe the parade of new technologies becoming available and old ones that appear to be dying. A technology's age is not what makes a media form succeed or fail. Technological newness doesn't explain why magazines, for example, are better positioned to flourish than are television networks; or why MP3 files, which sound worse than compact discs, are driving CDs to extinction. It doesn't explain why movies failed to kill off the novel or why bicycles outsell cars.

Technology only offers new possibilities, expanding the range of what we might *choose* to do, but it tells us nothing about what consumers will *want* to do after the novelty has worn off. When you finish reading, rather than walking across the room, you could choose to step aboard a Segway Personal Transporter and let its state-of-the-art technology roll you along. But I'd bet you won't. The technology is new and it's cool, but it won't take you where you want to go in the way you want to get there.

What matters is not merely new technologies but how consumers and businesses adapt those technologies to meet their own evolving needs. For that reason, to recognize the new choices that matter, we need a new way of thinking—and this book is your guide to that new perspective. We face not just one changing factor but four, interlinked and influencing one another in an ongoing, self-reflexive process: a shift in one factor influences the other three. Success in the new-media future depends on responding to all four factors simultaneously.

Does that sound complicated? It's no more so than driving a car. When you drive, you do at least four things at once: you control the speed and position of your car; you follow a route to a destination that you can't see in front of you; you remain aware of and react to the conditions of the road, including other cars moving alongside you; and you attend to your needs and those of your passengers. Any of these factors can change along the way, leading to further changes in the others; over the course of even a short trip, all four factors may change many times. Non-drivers often find this dynamic confusing or intimidating. Inept drivers may find it deadly. But for most of us, it becomes second nature.

This book guides you to that new way of thinking based on all four factors, preparing you to handle that car—or that virtual-reality spaceship—in the foreign yet still-familiar territory of our new-media future. These factors are transforming every kind of human communication that can be seen on a screen, heard on a speaker, or read from a page. That communication is key to business success, especially in this new world in which consumers listen more to one another than they do to marketing messages or to reviewers in the traditional media. As I will explain, the need for change showed itself first in traditional media industries and in those departments of non-media companies with obvious media functions—advertising, marketing, and public relations—yet, in time, those changes must spread to every department in every company. Every business is or must become a media business.

FOUR CHANGES AT ONCE

I found the seed for this book in 2005, when I became aware of all four of these factors operating on me at once. It happened while I was taking in a news story, something I did every day, yet the interplay of the four factors led me to change the way I got the story and reshaped my experience of getting the news. I had just started a job as the first president of digital media for CBS, and I was sitting in the front row at the CBS Affiliates meeting in Las Vegas, watching pilots of new CBS shows on a huge screen along with hundreds of station owners from around the country. To be honest, I was bored. I'd seen these previews several times already, but I was expected to sit in the front row with my boss, Leslie Moonves, and the other top CBS executives and watch them again.

My cell phone vibrated. It was a news alert in the form of a text message about the San Francisco 49ers. My son had worked for the team as an intern, and so I had them on my alert list. On my phone I read that my son's former boss, the team's longtime director of public relations, had been fired because he had made a sensitivity training film that was in bad taste. The *San Francisco Chronicle* had discovered the film and put video highlights on their website, SFGate. I read the headline, and then took out my BlackBerry to go to a couple of websites and see what I could learn. After reading details on SFGate.com and CNN.com, I emailed my son in Berlin, where he was interning for NFL Europe, to alert him. He emailed me back, saying he had already heard about the story and giving me more details. Then he asked me if I thought that a friend of his, a cameraman who had apparently appeared in the offensive video, was in trouble.

I emailed the news director, who was a friend of mine, at his station to see what I could find out. Then I used my BlackBerry web browser to read the Reuters and AP stories about the incident. After that, I pulled my cell phone back out and summoned V CAST, the television service, on which I watched a news report from CNN that showed portions of the offending video right there on my phone. A few minutes later, the news director replied, saying that my son's cameraman friend had asked his TV station for permission to appear in his one scene, and had no connection to the offensive material, so he was fine. I emailed my son with the good news.

When I looked up at the giant screen at the front of the room, the TV pilot that had lost my interest was still playing. In fifteen minutes, I had discovered a news story that mattered to me and satisfied my interest in it completely. I had even reported part of the story and advanced it beyond the public reporting, yet I'd never engaged with any traditional media in a conventional way. I had never even left my seat. For years, I'd been thinking about the separate factors reshaping media. Now here I felt all four at once. Why was that so important? I want to describe the significance of my personal experience; after that, I'll define the four factors in general.

I could get what I wanted when I wanted it. In the past, a consumer had to wait for the distributors of news, information, and entertainment to deliver the content as they chose. That gave the distributors great power—if you wanted the news, you had to be in front of your television at their scheduled time and you had to sit through the commercials. You had no choice. But I no longer had to wait to watch the evening news or to buy a copy of tomorrow's *San Francisco Chronicle.* Nor did I have to wait to get back to my office to check my phone messages. The convergence of text, image, audio, and video on my handheld devices made it all as available as I pleased, and I, the consumer, could choose when I saw and heard what.

I didn't pay for all the content I received. In the past, I would have paid for that news story by purchasing a paper, paying for my cable TV subscription, or taking in advertisements. Now all the usual financial arrangements were suspended. Although a small portion of my cell phone and BlackBerry subscription fees were shared with the organizations that published that news story, for the most part the existing business models failed to compensate the people who had done the reporting. The same technological convergence that made it so convenient for me to get the story also threatened the business model on which journalists, advertisers, public relations departments, authors, software engineers, and artists of all kinds depend. The old business models are doomed as they are based too heavily on delivery methods. The future belongs to the entrepreneurs who are building new models around creating the content that consumers want—and will pay to get.

What I needed was not just information, but help selecting and interpreting it. I had received that news alert in the middle of the day, like a "breaking news" interruption on television, but rather than relying on a TV editor to set my media priorities for me, I'd used a feature on the SFGate website that let me set alert priorities myself. There probably wasn't another person in that room who cared about that story, and none received it.

It's common to describe the information age as a shift from "scarcity" to "abundance," but most often what we experience is not a satisfying plenty—it's a potentially overwhelming tidal wave. If I wasn't going to drown in all of this new media, I needed a lot more help, through technological means like news aggregators, through peer recommendations such as social media, or through reinvented forms of traditional-media skills such as editorial guidance updated for the digital age. Curation could be as valuable as content.

That news story took a fresh form, and I was still discovering which forms I preferred. Once upon a time, a news "story" was an actual story spoken out loud by the town crier. Later, that story got printed on paper. Later still came radio and television versions, but still you knew what the story was: where it began and where it ended. By contrast, the version I got on that day was a hybrid—a mix of text messages, newspaper articles, video clips, and personal email. It mixed media and it mixed public and private sources. Overall, it was a new, unnamed form, fragmentary and lacking organization or control, but I preferred having the pieces now to having someone assemble the puzzle for me later.

And my preference for this new convergence of forms, a preference I turned out to share with many millions of other news readers and viewers, was a "vote" in favor of a change in how news stories were told. Yet this convergent form would not be the final one because I wasn't committed to this new form either. I'd keep testing the alternatives, the new ways to gather information that informs my personal and business decisions.

I saw that each existing form of media, from news stories to novels, from history textbooks to blogs to video games, would have to prove itself in ongoing competition with new multimedia hybrids. The winners will be whoever can transfer an idea, entertain an audience, shape an image, or sell a product in a more compelling way.

Here, then, are the four factors that together will shape our future:

1. *Consumers* choose what, how, and when they consume.
2. *Content* becomes king.
3. *Curation* cures information overload.
4. *Convergence* revolutionizes every form of communication.

However, presenting the four C's one by one hides the most important thing about these factors: they won't hold still. They won't wait for you or anyone to handle them one by one, any more than the other cars on the highway will hold still while you check your GPS navigator or make a phone call. Each factor keeps moving; instead of one change or even one series of changes, we have an ongoing cycle. This cycle of change is what sent traditional media into its death spiral—but this same cycle of change is opening up vast opportunities for those who can make use of new technologies, media forms, and relationships to communicate in new ways.

Earlier, I said that navigating this changed world was like a car trip, and that's true, but this trip is going to be longer, more perilous, and more surprising than any quick spin down the highway. What will it be like? It will resemble one of the great ocean voyages of discovery in the age of exploration, when captains and crew didn't know where they were going or what they would find when they got there. So they had to keep their eyes on the water and the weather and the stars; they had to be ready to defend themselves from pirates and to take help from friendly vessels when there was help to be had. They had to take in everything, all the changing qualities of the ocean spread before them. In the same way today, it's necessary to observe and understand all four C's as they reshape and reshape again the world around you. I call this world the *C-scape*.

The scale of change that businesses face is enormous, and the wreckage of companies that have not navigated the C-scape successfully are all around us. Blockbuster stayed with brick-and-mortar stores for delivering movies even while the consumer was shifting to digital; when it did attempt to match the Netflix approach, it was too late to prevent bankruptcy. General Motors didn't listen when consumers wanted smaller, more efficient cars. Quote.com was an early leader in financial news, with aggregated stock market news and information on the web. But it thought that pure aggregation, with no curation and no original content, would be enough to keep its unique users coming back. It is not a leader anymore.

Many business leaders are still unprepared to handle the complexities involved. Newspaper publishers routinely said that people didn't want to read news on computers, not least, they insisted, because men couldn't bring their computers into the john. Now it is too late for denial in the newspaper business, but many others seem to ignore the threats to their own industries. Like the heads of the airline and hotel industries, who still struggle to adapt to customers' increasing use of the Internet to book seats or rooms, leaders of traditional companies are not seizing the new opportunities that arise. Many are focused only on squeezing out a few more years of big salaries or remnant revenues the old way. Most are falling into the classic business errors that established organizations make at times of change, and their concentration on short-term performance jeopardizes their long-term hopes of renewal.

One example was the merger of America Online (AOL) and Time Warner. It became one of the world's most spectacular business failures, but it didn't have to be that way. When the merger was announced, it sounded like a winner. One of the world's foremost content companies was joining forces with a leading web portal that had millions of users on its platform. Traditional, top-quality content would meet new-media customers: it sounded like a perfect business model to me, until I realized that no one was making the necessary effort to blend the cultures of traditional and new media.

At AOL, new-media marketing dominated the business. The company had built an audience by sending out billions of free CD-ROMs to win over new dial-up Internet subscribers, but these marketers were selling digital delivery—connectivity to the web— not an editorial product. During most of AOL's existence, their customers had been forced to stay on the AOL platform by the technology that delivered their Internet access. But as is often the case, the new-media marketers knew more about building an audience than about maintaining a long-term relationship with that audience once it grew. The AOL people wrongly assumed that if people connected to the Internet through AOL, AOL owned them as customers forever. But as dial-up customers signed up for high-speed Internet connectivity, freeing them to reach other sites with ease, AOL could no longer keep them on the site.

The Time Warner people should have been an ideal source for that content. At Time Warner, content was king. Editors at the time had power comparable to that of publishers. They understood the value of their editorial content, but they didn't understand the value AOL might have added. AOL could have helped take their great brands—*Time,* CNN, HBO, *Fortune,* and *Sports Illustrated,* to name a few—to a new digital audience and could have done so just as many existing subscribers were already choosing to move to the convenience of the web. Instead, many executives at Time Warner regarded AOL as a waste of company money and time. Many resented the AOL team, who became rich while Time Warner's stock fell, and they feared that the AOL people would take over the entire company.

So the Time Warner executives froze out their new cousins and refused to work with them. It became widely known in the content world that it was easier to get a distribution deal with AOL if you were *outside* of Time Warner than if you were inside. The great brands of Time Warner put their content almost anywhere on the web but on AOL. And so, when AOL's delivery-based business model failed to maintain customer loyalty, there was no great, exclusive content to convince them to stay.

While companies like MarketWatch, iVillage, Drudge, and others grew huge audiences in demographic segments previously owned by Time Warner magazines—often with the help of partnerships with AOL, among others—the Time Warner print brands stagnated. Meanwhile, Time Inc. wasted hundreds of millions of dollars on their own web "portal," Pathfinder, causing one Time executive to proclaim that the company efforts were so spectacularly unsuccessful at building a real business that they had "redefined black hole."

The failure of that merger offers a what-not-to-do list for re-structuring a business in the media transition:

- They didn't recognize that AOL offered a new business model that could protect and expand the market for what they sold.
- They spurned the chance to take advantage of the savings that both the Internet and their partnership could provide.
- They missed the opportunity to instill in their consumers—who were new to the web and not yet set in their ways—new habits that would create new revenue streams.
- Rather than seizing the opportunity for a grand experiment, both sides of the company relied on their expectations and fears about how little the other side's approach could do for them—and these expectations were self-fulfilling.

What was missing? They had complementary content and technology and an existing content-hungry audience. What they lacked was leadership on both sides that was prepared to put old habits aside and build a convergent partnership based on satisfying their customers.

CONVERGENCE

The misunderstanding of "convergence" has dogged new media almost since the term was invented. In the early days, the digital revolutionary George Gilder famously predicted, "The computer industry is converging with the television industry in the same sense that the automobile converged with the horse, the TV converged with the nickelodeon, the word-processing program converged with the typewriter. . . ." To Gilder, media convergence meant the new would bury the old. But although Gilder was widely believed, he got it wrong. Media is far more than the technology it uses; every digital innovation is a version of its analog predecessors—nothing is ever as new as it seems—and every successful use of media now is a convergence between the possibilities of technology and the human needs that create business opportunities. It's often said in new-media circles that media has reached a Gutenberg moment, as revolutionary as the invention of the printing press. But so what? How does that matter? The obvious change is the profound disruption of our traditional ways of communicating and doing business—the vast disruptions and dangers of the C-scape. But the less obvious, more important change is a breathtaking democratization of opportunity. The costs of creating any kind of electronic media have never been lower; the traditional establishment has never been weaker or more in need of outside assistance; the range of new possible forms has never been greater. You don't need a special degree or the backing of a large corporation. The tools for exploring the new forms of media, like the tools for getting feedback about your attempts and for letting others know what you've found, are right there at hand, awaiting you.

In Part One, "The C-Scape: How Did We Get Here?" I guide you to recognize how each of the four factors have come into play, helping to train your eye, free you from outmoded habits of thought, and outfit you with the right questions to ask as you discover how the media transition changes business and everyday life for all of us. In Part Two, "What Happens to Markets?" I explain the impact of these changes on every stage of the marketing process, from advertising to customer service, to show which approaches will no longer work—and which strategies can replace them. Part Three, "What Happens to Products?" shows why every product is now a media product, and what that means for product design and development. Then in Part Four, "What Happens to Businesses?" I

THE C-SCAPE: HOW DID WE GET HERE?

THE FOUR FACTORS SHAPING THE C-SCAPE

If you strap an engine on a horse, do you have a car?

That question was put to me by my friend Dan Lagani, president of Reader's Digest Media. He was talking about plans by a consortium of magazine publishers to design and market their own e-reader for magazines. They knew that their traditional business—magazines printed on paper—was in trouble, and they were hoping to break into a new business by going digital and selling the hardware.

The trouble was that their e-reader seemed as if it had been designed by someone who didn't understand their business and the new challenges it faced. At the very moment Apple was about to unveil the iPad, their plan called for a black-and-white e-reader, something like the Amazon Kindle—but who wants to read magazines in black and white? Most of the magazine industry was built on the artful, attention-compelling mix of gorgeous photographs, colorful layout, and text. Who wants *Vogue* in black and white? Or even *Sports Illustrated*? Advertisers weren't going to like it as ads would look terrible. Even the resolution of the digital letters was worse than print in a magazine. No one was going to be able to relax with a version of their favorite magazine that gave them eyestrain.

And who wants a separate device just for magazines? Were we now expected to carry a phone, a book e-reader, and a magazine e-reader? Wasn't what consumers wanted more functions on fewer devices, not the other way around? The whole project made Lagani picture a group of horse-and-buggy drivers standing around, wishing to break into the automobile business, but not yet understanding how their world had changed or what business they were trying to be in. If you strap an engine on a horse, you still don't have a car.

Our conversation reminded me of the famous story about the railroad industry at the time that cars were first being mass-produced. As businesspeople often say, the industry's big mistake—and the reason that car companies replaced the railroad industry as the main source of transportation in the United States—was that the railroad barons didn't realize that they were not in the railroad business, they were in the transportation business. It's an important story, I think, because those railroad barons didn't do anything wrong—at least, not in the beginning. They had built up the railroad business, they were great at it, and they kept on doing it. What they didn't realize was that the world was changing around them. And as it changed, what they had provided so successfully lost its relevance to their customers.

Today, that's happening to all of us. Ultimately, every business moving through the C-scape is going to look around and realize we're not in Kansas anymore. In all of our travels, we've never seen any place that looks like where we are now—and it's still changing. Every business must ask itself what business it's in, and whether its traditional idea of how to be in that business (building railroads) is still relevant to what its customers actually want (convenient transportation).

But you can't solve a problem before you know what the problem is—otherwise, you'll just wind up putting engines on horses. The first step is to understand how the world is changing around you—the four C's that are transforming media, and through media, the world of business. Let's look at the factors that shape the C-scape.

1

THE FIRST FACTOR

CONSUMERS CHOOSE

Imagine you hear a song for the first time. You like it—so much, in fact, that you want to hear it again. So you go online, download it to whatever device suits you, take the song with you, listen wherever and whenever, as often as you like—and, perhaps most important, none of this seems surprising or unusual. That is the experience of consumer choice that many now take for granted. But while we may be comfortable with the speed, convenience, and freedom of choice afforded by new-media technologies, we often forget how revolutionary this is. Until recently, consumers' relationship to media was defined by the opposite of choice: passive waiting, inconvenience, and acceptance of whatever was offered. Not so long ago, if a new song was played on the radio and you wanted to hear it again, your only option was to sit by that radio and hope. New songs were provided to radio stations before their official release date to build excitement, so you couldn't buy them right away even if you wanted to; you might telephone the station and ask them to play it again, but the choice was theirs. Similarly, if you missed your favorite television program, you had to wait months until reruns were broadcast. Sometimes, the waiting and the planning required of consumers built anticipation, but more often, the experience was just frustrating. The power was in the hands of the media, and what they offered came on a take-it-or-leave-it basis. As at a concert, a play, or a sports event, you had only two choices: stay or go.

Actually, most of the new media forms of the twentieth century were even more one-sided than what had come before them. At least at a live performance, though you had no say about where or when it took place, you could make yourself heard. Live audiences could shout their feelings. If they lost patience and got up to leave, people noticed. They could demand an encore or wait afterward for the performers; they could talk to one another after the event ended. The oldest forms of entertainment and information—plays in an open amphitheater, games in the Coliseum, a town crier's announcements—provided plenty of "social networking." From that point of view, television and radio and the darkened movie theater were steps *backward*, non-interactive and isolating. As in the old Irving Berlin song, the consumer of much twentieth-century media was left "all alone by the telephone."

Now we're forgetting the old, dependent relationship of consumers on media providers, just as we're forgetting what used to be involved in research before the days of "search" on the web. Some leading-edge undergraduate libraries, including the University of Texas at Austin, contain no books (though other libraries on campus still exist). The prep school Cushing Academy in New England has no library books at all, only e-readers. Library space is now used for "virtual learning environments" where students conduct multimedia research, rows of desks have access to electrical outlets for laptops, and study groups can meet for face-to-face "interactivity." Books still considered relevant have been moved to other libraries on campus. (In the film *All the President's Men*, there is an unforgettable scene where the journalists working on the story of the Watergate scandal search through thousands of slips of paper in the Library of Congress. Would a young audience today even know what the journalists are doing?)

POWER SHIFTS TO THE CONSUMER

This shift began not in the 1990s, with the widespread use of the personal computer or the Internet, but in 1950, with the introduction of a game-changing technology, one that would revolutionize how every business was conducted and touch all of our lives— the remote control. To be honest, it wasn't impressive at first. A small box connected by a bulky cable to your television, it incorporated no cutting-edge technology. The basic design came from the German military, which had used it to control motorboats. The first civilian use was in garage-door openers. It had only two buttons, one for "up" and one for "down," yet while it doesn't seem like much today, this first remote control did something new and crucial when it was hooked up to a television. It gave viewers a new choice, one with enormous implications for the future.

Until then, if you were sitting in your chair watching television and you wanted to change the channel, you had to climb out of the chair, walk across the room, and turn the channel by hand. To browse through available shows, you either had to make multiple trips back and forth across the room, or you had to stand up beside the television while you scanned the different shows. All the inertia of fatigue, habit, and laziness pushed for watching whichever channel happened to be on. The networks designed their shows with that inertia in mind: their goal was to make shows that were inoffensive— not great shows, just shows not bad enough to drive you away. It was as if the networks followed a kind of psychological version of Newton's second law of thermodynamics: objects at rest tend to stay at rest, especially if they've just had a long workday and have finally gotten comfortable sitting down. So secure were that era's network executives that they had no direct contact with their audience at all. They left the minor problem of the audience and its preferences to the local broadcast stations, confident that viewers would behave as expected—after all, the viewers didn't have much choice.

Then, in 1950, the Zenith Radio Corporation introduced the "Lazy Bone" remote control, and the old balance of power between producers and consumers—or, perhaps, the balance of laziness—began to shift. Now a viewer could change channels without getting up; people began to change the channel. However, the cultural landslide did not start overnight. Consumers didn't like that cable running across their floor. They tended to trip over it. Adoption of the Lazy Bone was slow. So Zenith developed the "Flash-matic," the first wireless remote, which required the viewer to shine a flashlight (the remote) at one of four photocells at the corners of the TV screen. Each corner controlled a different function. With the Flash-matic, there was no more danger of remote-control-related injury, but on sunny days the television sometimes changed channels at random or switched itself on and off.

Next came the "Space Command" remote control, in 1956, which used ultrasound waves to solve the technical problems of earlier versions. It was far more reliable but also more expensive: the six extra vacuum tubes required in a Space Command television raised its price by almost a third. So although ultrasound technology set the standard for the next thirty years of remote controls, what we now call channel surfing remained a luxury of the wealthy until the 1960s, when transistors replaced vacuum tubes and brought down prices for most electronics. At that point, with both convenience and price within reach, more than 9 million television-watching households bought transistor-based remote controls. The era of media choice began.

How much difference did that remote make? Over time, it became clear to the network executives that producing an inoffensive show was not good enough. Now, instead of committing to one channel, often for the night, viewers could move around, making one network's show the top program at seven o'clock and another network's show the winner at eight. The networks were now motivated to make shows exciting enough to poach viewers from rival channels.

Not only did consumers now have an easier time making choices, but the nature of these choices changed as they gained more influence. To a small degree, they began to share in the decisions of the producer. The "technological convergence" of the armchair and the television by means of the remote control not only brought a greater variety of programming into the home, it brought a degree of respect and attention along with it. Producers had to place themselves a little more at the level of consumers, asking: Who are they? What would they like? It was a slight leveling of a still-very-uneven playing field—an unhappy viewer in the 1960s got a lot more response by yelling at actors on a stage than by angrily switching channels—but it was a start.

Further innovations brought new choices for consumers—changes not only in the *number* of choices available but in the *nature* of those choices, and the balance of power that defined the relationship between consumers and producers of television shifted again. In 1976, the video cassette recorder was introduced, first the Betamax format and then the more successful VHS cassette. For the first time, powers that had been the sole preserve of the television networks—the power to own a copy of a program and thus the power to decide when and how often it would be shown—were also in consumers' hands. The fast-forward button made it possible to speed through television advertisements. The video rental store gave consumers a selection of programming not controlled by the networks, and the camcorder made it possible to create one's own programming at home. These developments are well known, but even those who lived through them were not aware of the underlying existential convergence: how the producers and the consumers of video were becoming not just more equal in power but more similar to each other. The video generation found it far easier than before to learn and participate in the basic skills of moviemaking; the yawning gap between film professionals and amateurs continued to close. And then in 1999, digital video cameras and Apple's iMovie editing software made it possible to create a professional-quality digital movie or music video at home.

Again, though, the technology took time to mature. Video cassette recorders were hard to use; if you didn't program the clock correctly or if a power outage erased the setting, the clock readout would flash on and off. All over the world VCRs flashed the wrong time all day and night. One study at Yale University found that only 42 percent of adults presented with a VCR and a manual could follow the instructions successfully; many people won't read a manual at all. Within the industry, it was accepted that as many as 80 percent of VCR owners couldn't program their VCRs to record and only used them to play. Older viewers often asked their children to handle the awkward technology for them. It was a skill that required not only a little technical knowledge, but also some patience and some ongoing attention to schedules. As a result, many fewer shows were recorded than was technologically possible. I remember in the early days of the VCR I knew one person who set his machine to tape *Late Night with David Letterman* after he went to bed, so he could watch it over breakfast the next morning. Out of all my friends, he was the only one with the interest and the dedication to do that every night.

More signs of a dramatic shift in power were clear in 1980, when pay television was introduced with the arrival of cable service. Once again, consumers discovered not just new choices of what to watch but new choices in their relationship with television producers. The interruptions of programs by sponsor advertisements, which had been obligatory, became optional: if you preferred, you could choose to pay a monthly bill. The content restrictions on language and sexual situations also became optional because no government license was required for cable broadcast, as opposed to broadcast over the airwaves.

One marker of the deeper changes under way in the relationship of consumer to producer was the way these new television networks named themselves. The traditional networks had given themselves names that showcased their size and power. ABC: American Broadcast Company. NBC: National Broadcast Company. By contrast, the new cable stations organized and named themselves in terms of the consumer they intended to serve: CNN, the Cable News Network, offered news whenever you wanted it. ESPN, the Entertainment and Sports Programming Network, offered twenty-four-hour sports. HBO, Home Box Office, was a round-the-clock movie box office in your home. None of these channels gave you exactly the show you wanted, but they could promise a show in the right category at any time of day or night.

The true extent of these changes started to become clearer with the introduction of digital video recorders such as TiVo in 2000. With digital video recording devices, it was not only possible, with effort, to refuse many of the remaining obligations of the ordinary viewer—to watch shows on the networks' schedule, to watch the advertisements—it was easy. Viewers could program the shows they wanted in their own order and catch up at their own pace if they fell behind—which meant that they could feel relaxed about postponing almost any show. Some viewers entirely gave up watching shows at the time they were scheduled, and although this threw the networks' relationships with their sponsors into chaos, it went on. Our relationship to television, now far from one of dependence and powerlessness, had become more like the relationship to a butler: it comes when we call and it brings us what we want, when we want it. Also like a butler, TiVo could "suggest" shows by highlighting other programming in the same category as a show you watched previously.

These shifts from dependence to choice have formed a new set of expectations whose effects continue to mushroom, effects no business can ignore. To retain consumer loyalty, businesses must respect that consumers now both have and expect:

- **More choices in every category, accessed more easily.** Computers and smartphones have shifted the balance of laziness in the relationship between customers and the businesses they patronize, becoming the "remote controls" that provide the choice to buy products and services at the touch of a button. It used to be an advantage to be the local retailer, but now, as not just book stores and music stores, but hardware, drug, grocery stores, and others have learned, local is anywhere that delivers.

- **More kinds of choices.** Consumers expect increasing choice not just about when and how their content is delivered, but in an increasing variety of features. eBay and other sites that facilitate the sale of secondhand goods have made "newness" an optional feature—you can buy almost any product now with or without "newness" included.

- **Greater ease of use.** Consumers often prefer the product that is more convenient or more intuitive to use, even if it isn't the highest possible quality. Sony wagered that its Betamax video-tape format, which was first to market, would beat the VHS format, which gave an inferior picture but held more hours of programming. But Sony lost the bet—consumers preferred the convenience of a tape that held a full eight hours of pro-gramming even if the picture suffered. Then the entire televi-sion industry doubted the DVD because it only played video; it couldn't record. Yet consumers found it easier to use a tech-nology that didn't make them wait while they rewound or fast-forwarded: they turned away from tapes and chose the DVD.

- **The choice not to commit.** That consumers can access a new technology or a new form of information or entertainment does not mean they will; even when they do, as their freedoms in-crease, they expect to have the option not to make a full com-mitment. The music website Lala offered fans not just the usual options of buying the whole CD or downloading individual MP3 files, but also the choice of listening to a song streamed exactly once (for free) or as often as they liked, but only on the company's website (for ten cents). The site was purchased by Apple for a reported $80 million, with the expectation that Apple would adapt Lala's cloud-based approach for an upcom-ing version of iTunes. Zipcar rents cars by the hour for those who don't want to commit for a full day, let alone lease or make a purchase. These and other new businesses are based on offer-ing the chance to make a smaller-than-traditional commitment.

- **An increasing sense of entitlement.** Choices that seem new and experimental one year become familiar—then essential. Music downloading, for example, which began as a high-tech novelty, became a requirement. When the music industry didn't offer a download option, consumers learned to do it for themselves, illegally. When the BBC and CNET, among others, were slow to create smartphone apps for their news products, unauthorized designers created their own—and pocketed the one-time revenue for selling them. As each new generation is offered choice, their standards go up, and businesses must respect those new standards.

Consumer choice sounds like a simple, one-dimensional idea—consumers used to have less choice, now they have more—but it is more complex. Yet as complex as it can be, managing it requires businesses to do only two things:

- Offer consumers the increasing range of choices they expect.
- Learn to observe, closely and frequently, which choices consumers of certain types or in specific areas and markets choose, and adjust their offerings accordingly.

So far, few businesses have done both well. Traditional companies have tended to underestimate the enthusiasm for convenience and freer choice—television networks didn't anticipate the havoc that digital video recorders would wreak; newspaper and magazine publishers insisted that computers and handheld devices could not replace paper. But while traditional media have been consistently caught unaware, new-media organizations tend to overestimate how thoroughly and how quickly consumers will give up the old for the new. In the last fifteen years, there have been endless declarations on the new-media side about the death of this or that older technology—"no one reads anymore," "television is dead," "everything from now on will be interactive"—and yet, as we will see in the coming chapters, many traditional forms remain quite healthy even when their traditional providers are not: to take one example, viewing of "appointment television," meaning shows watched in the old-fashioned way, on the screen of a physical television and at the time when they are scheduled, has continued to *increase*, according to Nielsen, reaching 153 hours per month in 2008—even as time-shifted television and interactive video are also on the rise. Interactive entertainment may be the hot new thing, but we still watch the Super Bowl in record numbers. Yet, as Chris Anderson explained in *The Long Tail,* most big hits are smaller than they were before the Internet: the audience for television is divided into so many niches that viewership for single shows is down. Television is not dying—it is learning to live with a disaggregated audience that can enjoy its increased video options and not commit.

As power is shared more evenly between producer and consumer, success in managing consumer choice depends on giving up the habits of the old uneven power relationship and forming a new, more equal relationship. That might mean giving up hammering at an audience with relentless advertising and instead shifting to surveys about their preferences and priorities. It means less "staying on message" and more listening—and responding with substantive changes a consumer can see, such as switching to "green" packaging materials when your customers start to blog about their environmental concerns.

2

THE SECOND FACTOR

CONTENT BECOMES KING

Subscribers to the *Washington Post* in the early 2000s received almost a dollar's worth of free paper every week. That was because the price per issue was nearly a dollar less than the cost of the paper used to print it. The ink, the printing, the delivery, and the actual reporting of the news were not covered by the subscription price. By contrast, the *New York Times* was both thinner and more expensive—as *Slate* editor Michael Kinsley quipped, "[The *Times*] might even have a viable business model if it could sell the paper with nothing written on it."

Newspapers literally weren't worth the paper they were printed on, yet for decades, of course, both the *Post* and the *Times* had viable businesses, for two reasons. First, there was revenue from what was bundled into a newspaper along with the news: commercial advertisements, classified advertisements, movie listings (accompanied by movie advertisements), coupons, inserted brochures, and so on. Second, newspaper subscribers were a captive audience. Printing presses were expensive to buy and to run, and economies of scale favored a bigger, established paper over upstarts. Even if a newcomer could create better news, it couldn't afford to print and deliver competitively. No consumer had more than a few choices of newspaper, and those few local papers tended to segment themselves according to geography, ideology, or demographics to guarantee themselves a captive audience. If you wanted to read the news every day, you had little choice but to subscribe to the local monopoly. The number of pages of international reporting delivered to your door was determined not by subscribers' love of exceptional journalism, but by the number of guys listing their Mustangs for sale and the ability of big stores to buy catalog inserts, but readers didn't give it much thought.

DELIVERY NO LONGER DELIVERS

While nostalgia may nudge some of us to see media's present financial crisis as the chaotic collapse of a once great, solid, and rational system, the truth is that the old business models that paid for traditional media were always jury-rigged, technology-specific accidents of history, based on delivering quirky and expensive materials to a captive audience. The entire system of television networks and local broadcast stations, for example, came about because television signals degrade in the air. To deliver the signal across the country, it was necessary to have many local broadcast stations to boost the signal, and each one provided some local programming and got the rest from the networks.

Similar arrangements held in other media for similar reasons, specifically the cost of physical delivery: the long-playing record album, for example, forced consumers to buy ten or twelve songs when they might have wanted only a few, because no one could press a record for them with just the songs they wanted. The required textbook, for many years, had to be purchased whether the professor assigned the entire book or only a chapter, because no one could set up a new publishing company just to service the needs of one class.

In all of these cases, to access the content they wanted, consumers depended on various middlemen. They wanted the news stories, but they paid the paper suppliers and the printer and the unionized truckers. They wanted the television shows, but they paid for the nationwide system of broadcast stations, and for the networks' system of developing and then scrapping dozens of pilot programs to find a few big hits. Then came the Internet, the mother of all disintermediating technologies, making it possible for buyers and sellers to find each other without most of those middlemen. One by one, the Internet and the other new delivery technologies broke the old supply chains across media.

In the news business, search engines broke the near-monopoly of the local newspaper, putting every English-language newspaper on the web in competition with the rest. Now not only could consumers often get what they wanted from the paper without paying for the old delivery methods, they could choose among hundreds of different papers and cherry-pick the coverage they liked best, story by story. At the same time, many advertisers discovered that they too could get what they wanted without paying for paper, printing, and trucks. Free advertising online replaced the classified advertising that had supported the old newspaper business. If you want to know who killed newspapers, the culprit wasn't just Google; it was Craigslist, too.

How will the media rebuild its delivery-based business models? It won't. The captive audience has escaped. Consumers have little reason to pay for delivery that isn't digital anymore, and digital delivery doesn't create comparable monopolies to support content. In the transitional era, as Jeff Zucker, head of NBC Universal, famously said, everyone in media is worried that in giving up the old analog delivery models for digital replacements, they will "end up trading analog dollars for digital pennies."

That's not just a problem for people who work in media. It's a problem for anyone with eyes and ears. The old system funded much of the content we love—not just great journalism but movies, music, television, literature, and so on. As those profits disappear, so does support for developing new ideas, art, and entertainment. Our amazing new powers to access what's already out there tend to overshadow this problem, but despite bloggers and despite the speed and convenience of the Internet, most news still comes from newspaper journalists, and newspaper journalists are running out of jobs. In general, since it emerged, new media has been cannibalizing the expensive original content once fed by the traditional media business model. The corpse won't last forever.

The hope has been that a new business model will be media's salvation. But if there is an all-purpose business model for media, no one has found it—and I don't believe anyone will. This pessimism is not because the business of media is hopelessly changed, but because in some ways it remains as it was. The business models for traditional media, such as the bundle of different sorts of advertising that kept newspapers profitable, were accidents that varied according to the specific medium—radio, remember, had no classified ads. I believe the answer will again be a patchwork of partial solutions specific to the kind of content being delivered, and the habits and preferences of the particular audience that wants it. Just as in the past, in the future there will be no one solid and rational system, but rather a collection of improvised arrangements based on lucky alignments of buyers' and sellers' needs.

To find them, those in media and in business generally must shift their thinking in the following ways:

- **Learn to make it in consumers' interest to pay for content**. When Apple launched iTunes, the conventional wisdom held that "young people won't pay for music anymore," as they'd grown used to downloading it for free. And while iTunes hasn't solved all the problems of the music industry, it made paying for music cool again by offering a stylish "one-button" solution. (At the time, MP3 players were in part a way to show you were enough "in the know" to get your music for free.) Just as the Internet wasn't widely adopted until broadband connections eliminated the need to call your provider on a telephone modem and wait to be connected, the iPod and iTunes took downloading mainstream by making it easy to get content, easy to organize that content, and easy to pay for it. (In the same way, millions now pay a monthly subscription fee for the ease of a digital video recorder such as TiVo, even though they could record the same shows for free on a VCR.)

  In addition, iPod's distinctive interface—the sleek player with its white ear buds, so different from the bulky CD Walkman—meant that you were paying not just for a more convenient technology but for a more attractive lifestyle choice. Women especially seemed more willing to be seen wearing an iPod than a CD Walkman. In other words, the decline of the old business models has brought producers and consumers closer in yet another way: they must engage in an ongoing negotiation about how content is going to get paid for and what would make paying for it feel worthwhile.

  Some of this is a matter of education. Consumers are already paying in ways they don't realize—portions of cable and satellite subscription fees, as well as cell phone subscription fees, go to creating the content that appears on those devices. Consumers pay for networks such as Lifetime, USA, CNN, Fox News, or the Golf Channel, but they don't even know how much. It's just part of a bundled bill. Educating consumers on how accepting new business models will get them the high-quality content they want is as important a part of success as creating that content.

- **Stop asking what new sales model will support the existing business and put content first.** Ask the big question: what sort of business organization will support sales of your content? I hear frequent discussion in the industry of what the *New York Times* can do to replace its past revenue stream so it can pay its current salaries to management and retain its current building in Midtown Manhattan. That gets the problem backwards. The right question is whether high salaries for management and impressive real estate help create and sell the best news content in the world. And from the biggest conglomerate to the smallest start-up, some version of this question applies to every business out there.

- **Take advantage of all the ways that the Internet and other digital technologies can lower costs.** Digital technologies have lowered costs and barriers to entry in every area. Whether a company is in the business of creating and selling text, images, audio, video, or a multimedia hybrid, the expenses have been dramatically lowered for those willing to give up some of their traditional methods. At the same time, the Internet makes available essentially cost-free content such as reader photos and video, blogs, wiki-sources, customer evaluations, and so forth. For businesses in general, these represent free sources of market research and quality assurance information. Does the product work? Would consumers buy more if the features were changed or the quality was improved? All this information is being offered for free to companies willing to listen. Businesses tend to become aware of amateur media when they become a threat: Kryptonite had to pay attention to YouTube when a now-famous video showed how to pick one of their bicycle locks with a ballpoint pen cap. But companies need to view amateur media not just as potential threats but as natural resources to be harvested, as many retail websites have done by encouraging customers to post reviews, which, when positive, build confidence in the retailers' products. They can take advantage of the same freedoms and opportunities that the technical convergence offers consumers.

- **Keep experimenting with business models.** In any business, when it comes to collecting revenue there are only three basic flavors. Payment can be collected
  a. Unit by unit
  b. By longer-term subscription
  c. From advertisers

These approaches can also be combined. The traditional newspaper was offered for sale both by subscription and at the newsstand and was bundled with various forms of advertising; in searching for content-based equivalents, it's necessary to experiment with many possible combinations and hybrids. The fashion industry has always discounted high-end merchandise to clear out excess inventory. Yet if all that merchandise was offered at a discount online from the beginning, it would undercut full-price retail sales. Instead, a number of websites such as Gilt. com have sprung up to offer "sample sales" on the Internet in a carefully restricted way: one designer's merchandise goes on sale for a thirty-six hour period beginning at lunch hour. Shoppers who could never have reached the physical site of a sample sale at lunch can shop from their desks, but because the selection is limited to one designer and the period of the sale is so short, it's unlikely that this online discount shopping will undercut sales to customers who would go to the physical stores. It's an example of a new online revenue stream based on the specific content and the specific habits of one group of consumers.

- **Don't trust predictions and conventional wisdom; experiment.** Predictions about what business models consumers will accept are regularly wrong. "Micro-payments," such as paying a few cents for a single article, were supposed to save the newspaper industry, but consumers couldn't be convinced to pay for what they were already finding for free, and the World Wide Web Consortium halted its efforts to develop standards for microtransactions. At the same time, the subscription model for television was widely doubted, and many in television expected cable subscriptions to drop substantially during the recession of 2008; yet they didn't. Don't look for the one magic bullet. Instead, take a "beta" approach: find as many promising approaches as you can, try them all, and see what works in practice.

The biggest obstacles to finding viable new business models are not technological, they are mental. To one degree or another, we are all stuck in the old way of thinking—there is simply too much new out there for anyone to anticipate the significance of all of it every time. So we go on worrying about the future of newspapers, even though, as Clay Shirky put it, "We don't need newspapers. We need journalism."

3

THE THIRD FACTOR

CURATION CURES INFORMATION OVERLOAD

What makes the C-scape so challenging is that one aspect of business may change drastically while another remains as it was. Go back four hundred years, for example, to the businesspeople in Shakespeare's play *The Merchant of Venice*. They don't seem all that different from businesspeople today. They put their money into seagoing vessels carrying valuable cargo, and while the ships are at sea, they worry that those ships might wreck in a storm or be raided by pirates, and their expensive cargo lost. Even with centuries separating us, we can recognize those merchants as investors. Yet while their business concerns are familiar, their methods of gathering news and information seem primitive. With no way to contact the ships, they can do nothing more effective than walking up and down on the Rialto Bridge in Venice, asking passing travelers if they've heard any news. The first words of the third act of the play are: "Now, what news on the Rialto?" A merchant gets news about a ship, but immediately he starts to worry that what he's heard may only be gossip. The scarcity of good information is his constant problem: how to get more—and more accurate—news.

Jump ahead to 1989. The novelist Saul Bellow made headlines with a speech at Harvard's Kennedy School of Government in which he complained that if anyone attempted to read the entire Sunday *New York Times,* "It would, if you could do it, constipate your intelligence for a long time to come." Now, instead of a scarcity of news, there was too much to process, too much information coming in from all corners of the globe. The problem was no longer just how to get more good information but how to prevent being overwhelmed by it.

How widespread that anxiety has become was revealed when Yahoo tried to challenge Google for dominance in web searching. It came up with a slogan—"Are you getting lost in the links?"— that didn't promise that Yahoo was faster or more accurate or better for searching in any practical way. Their sole selling point offered to soothe a Google user's fear that a Google search gives us too much: we feel lost. In the media transition, the most popular earphones you could invent wouldn't help us to hear better, they would screen out all we don't want to hear in the first place.

To get earphones like that, you have to change your approach. Bellow made an assumption that no longer applies: that if he was going to understand his world, he was obligated to read the entire newspaper alone and think through it by himself. But in the C-scape there are new ways to get help—from computers, from experts, or from peers. There are online content aggregators, many of them automated, such as sites that gather specific categories of news stories from around the web about a specific person, place, or topic. And yet, while aggregation saves time in searching, on its own it doesn't solve the problem Bellow described. It makes it worse: the more information aggregated for me to read, the more time I spend reading.

MANAGING INFORMATION OVERLOAD

Traditional media offered some help with information overload in the form of human beings who specialized in sorting better from worse, significant from trivial, clear from murky: namely, editors. News editors, for example, chose which stories were important enough to put on the front page or to lead off the broadcast, which ones got a lot of space and time and resources, and which only got a brief mention. Now, with the explosion of amateur media—blogs, online discussion forums, social networking sites—we have moved from information scarcity through information abundance to information overwhelm. Even as traditional media sources decline, the same explosion of choice that threatens to kill them off has intensified our need for the human guidance that those forms used to provide.

This explains the explosive growth of "curated" online media aggregators such as the Huffington Post. The website links to scoops of current news, other stories in a variety of categories, blogs, video, and reader comments, selecting what the site's editors guess will matter most to its audience and prioritizing them by category. Like a newspaper, it has a "front page" where it describes itself as "The Internet Newspaper." The front page changes throughout the day, mainly offering links to the outside news sources that provide most of the content. It also offers a small amount of original content, often aimed at interpreting the news for the liberal reader. The site's unique visitors number in the tens of millions.

HuffPost took off during the 2008 presidential campaign. Left-leaning readers could check in day or night to find the latest campaign-related news, prioritized not according to the traditional rules of journalism that aspired to neutrality, but according to what those readers were most likely to find compelling, from gossip to polls to new campaign issues, from hard news to scandals to personality profiles. More than just a clearinghouse for information about the campaign and its larger context, it was a curated emotional smorgasbord, arranged to feed the hopeful, nervous, halfway-addicted voter wondering, *How are we doing right now?* This media smorgasbord is a world away from Shakespeare's uninformed investors, walking the Rialto starved for information. Yet it's not as far as it may seem from Saul Bellow in the 1980s, reading the *Times* from front to back and trying to make sense of it on his own. Bellow was already relying on a high-quality, curated news aggregator, in an analog form based on the hardy technology known as paper—his news aggregator was called the *New York Times*. Although he refused the editors' suggestions about which stories in its pages were most important, he still relied on them to select the stories included in the selection of the news of the day— he relied on them to select "all the news that's fit to print," as the paper's slogan promised. The change from then to now is in the increased pressure on our attention and the increased help that is available. Every consumer-facing business today must understand that it is contributing to that unpleasant and sometimes unmanageable pressure: its advertisements, its press releases, and its cultivated mentions on television or in print—in fact, all its attempts to build a brand or shape a public perception through the media— come rushing at the consumer as part of this overwhelming flood. Any or all of these communications may feel like part of a problem. To solve that problem, consumers rely on curation—other people to sort out what is important, whom to believe, and what it means.

AMATEURS FIND THEIR VOICES

The biggest shock for those used to traditional media has been how many people, when selecting curators, don't draw that line where traditional media has always expected it: between the reliable word of professionals and the unvetted remarks of amateurs. Rather than turning exclusively to paid editors such as the staffs at the Huffington Post or the *New York Times* and the professional writers whose work they link to, people seem content to have their thinking assisted by people with no formal qualifications at all, from bloggers who mark ideas and entertainment as important by linking it to their blogs, to anonymous peers posting ratings and reviews, to YouTube users who post whatever video they think someone else might watch for a few seconds.

Consider the experience of Answers.com, an information aggregator that gathers facts from 150 different vetted encyclopedias and other reference sources to answer users' questions. A successful site for many years, one of the top fifty for traffic in the world, its staff found that growth in page views was leveling off, and so it launched WikiAnswers.com, where users of the site could add their own responses to factual questions. Growth on that site has been astronomical—they found, as so many journalists and expertise-oriented sites have done, that many people prefer an answer cobbled together by non-experts to one certified by professionals. To someone thinking in the traditional-media paradigm, this scenario doesn't make any sense. Why would anyone seeking information prefer guesses and uninformed guidance to real expertise? Many people in the traditional news business continue to wonder, why would anyone go to a blog when they could read a trained journalist? Why would a potential consumer for a product trust amateur ratings over *Consumer Reports*?

In some cases, the explanation is that the amateur immersed in a world knows it better than a professional; I know sailors who make a game of spotting the factual errors in professional writing about sailing. But that doesn't explain the explosion of reliance on bloggers, message boards, chat rooms, and the like. The explanation requires another shift in thinking, away from a focus on the traditional functions of the producer (delivering more information) and toward the new needs of the consumer coping with overwhelm.

Imagine I'm going to have friends over for dinner. I want to buy some wine, although wine, let's say, is not something I know much about. On an expert site, I can learn what is considered the best wine to pair with the food I want to serve. But will I like that wine? Will my guests like that wine? I don't want to serve a "wrong" wine, but I don't want something that may be "correct" but that none of my guests likes. Nor do I want a wine that tastes good but seems pretentious sitting on my table, given who I am and how I live. I can collect all the expert advice I want, but it won't help me unless I know how that information fits with my community and my sense of myself. And in terms of overwhelm, when I go to a website that provides expert factual knowledge, I may leave feeling worse off than when I arrived: now I have *even more information* to cope with than before. Expertise, in this way, is like new technology: even if it's perfectly correct, I may not know how to "operate" it to suit my life. If your business relies on experts to validate your product or service, it's time to reconsider how you present that expertise.

The problem is made more complicated because there is so much expertise out there. For any given question, there are likely to be a range of expert recommendations. If I have a baby who won't sleep through the night, I can find experts who will instruct me on why and how I should leave the baby alone to cry herself to sleep. I can find other experts who advocate bringing the baby to sleep in the parents' bed. I can find still more experts who are somewhere in the middle, who suggest separating from the baby at night but in slower and gentler ways. With so much information a mouse click away, almost every search leads to a range of experts. Often what I need to know before I can use any of their expertise is more about myself and my community, meaning the people I trust. What would people just like me do? I could figure that out myself, but so often time is exactly what I don't have.

Peer sites let me delegate questions of that kind, which can protect me from much of what is overwhelming about the new-media nation—and for that reason, the non-expert source may answer my deeper questions, even if it sometimes gets the facts wrong. People have always asked family and friends for this kind of imperfect but comfortable assistance, but today family and friends may be distant, while the computer and the smartphone are close at hand.

Does this mean the end of professional expertise? No. WikiAnswers was a runaway success, but the expertise-based Answers. com remains a huge draw as well. The important lesson is not that amateur always beats professional but that what consumers want is not, necessarily, more information. They want to find the information they need without drowning in it. They want to get on with their lives. Curated sources with a clear slant, political or otherwise, are not *alternatives* to blogs, chat rooms, or other amateur sources. They are professional versions of the same service, making the same promise: not just "we know what you don't" but also "we think and feel like you do"—so leave some of your thinking to us.

In an interview about the Huffington Post's political slant during the Obama–McCain campaign, Arianna Huffington said, "We are opposed to the war in Iraq. We think the troops should come home. The headlines are going to reflect what is in the best interests of the country." Her remark is telling because it doesn't make clear if the "we" to whom she refers is her staff or her target readers—and that's the power of its appeal. Right or wrong, they know how their users want their politics served.

Of course, no site can do all its visitors' thinking for them, and even the best will guess wrong some of the time. But on the web, information can be self-correcting. The stories that get read most are moved to more visible places on the site, and unpopular stories are removed. Most sites adapt to the preferences expressed by readers through mouse clicks. Digital curators, unlike their analog predecessors, can collaborate with their audience in real time, using their own responses to bring the site closer to the reader's desire for a community that understands how he or she thinks. The combination of technological convergence and human editors leads to a convergence of news source and audience. This is a new role for media, a different kind of trust, and while it may alarm some in traditional media, we are heading that way.

For businesses, the lesson is that instead of speaking directly to consumers, one to one, as in advertising, they must join the larger conversation that curators provide on their sites. Businesses have less control over conversations about their products and services than in the past, when consumers were offered advertisements to which they could only respond yes or no. Nor can they always influence consumers by influencing particular authorities—the journalist who covers their industry, the reviewer who stays in their hotel or eats in their restaurant. What consumers trust has changed: instead of the expert reviewer, they may want to hear from the source—the person who stayed in the room, who ate the meal, or who first drove the new model car. Just as viewers have come to demand "reality" programming on television, pushing aside traditional scripted shows with professional actors, some consumers of all products now demand "reality" advertising and "reality" public relations, provided by people just like them.

But while this shift represents a loss of traditional forms of influence and control that businesses have relied on, there is great opportunity here as well:

- **Lowered marketing costs.** Customers who like to talk about what they buy are a gold mine because the way to reach future customers is through existing customers. And just like "reality television," when compared with the traditional scripted kind, social networks that businesses join or host are dramatically less expensive than traditional scripted advertising with paid actors.

- **Larger, better-targeted audiences.** One of the frustrations for marketers in the media transition is that it's less and less possible to reach enormous audiences, as those audiences have so many choices within smaller niche-oriented groups. Popular curated sites, however, gather like-minded people together, reaggregating the audiences not just in greater numbers but also according to their interests and habits. A study by Anderson Analytics found that Twitter users are more likely to be interested in sex than the average Facebook, MySpace, or LinkedIn user, and more enthusiastic as well about news, restaurants, sports, politics, personal finance, and religion; LinkedIn users are more likely to read about soap operas online; MySpace users tend not to exercise. Gathering such data on the users of large sites offers marketers some of the advantages of the old blockbuster audiences combined with greater selectivity: a new hybrid approach, offering businesses access to a mass audience targeted for advertisers by interest.

- **A new value proposition to offer consumers, clients, partners, and suppliers.** Even if someone owns a needle, it's worthless if it remains lost in the haystack. The magnet that pulls it out is as necessary—and as valuable—as the needle itself. In the same way, curating content is often as valuable as the content itself. Or, to put it another way: you can add value and command loyalty by becoming a reliable, trustworthy curator, or by creating gathering places for conversations that your audience trusts. That's what HuffPost did for its readers and what Visa Business Network did for its small-business clients.

MANAGING SOCIAL OVERLOAD

It's not only information that grows overwhelming. New technology also presents us with what can be an overwhelming amount of social contact. We can travel so easily, meet so many people, and keep in touch with all of them—but who has time? Just as aggregation and curation save time in our relationship to ideas and opinions, social networking sites offer similar help with social relationships. While some critics see the progression from email, instant messaging, and text messaging to MySpace and Facebook, among others, and then to Twitter as a series of self-indulgent fads, they share a practical goal: to manage the ever-growing list of contacts better.

Not that long ago, the only quick way to communicate was the telephone. Yet, although it seemed quick compared to the letter, it still required time and coordination of schedules: your only choices were either to get the other person to come to the phone or to leave a message that required a response and perhaps another call. Both parties on a call had to interrupt whatever else they were doing, and once they were on the phone together, they had various social conventions to uphold—"How are you?" "I'm fine," and so on. Although most people take it for granted now, email, texts, and instant messages reduced the amount of time we spend on some kinds of communication by minimizing most of those formal conventions and banishing the need for simultaneous conversation. They also provided a permanent, searchable record of what was said.

Facebook took the process even further, making it polite to communicate with many friends or colleagues at once. (No more emails beginning, "Sorry for the mass email!") It provided a substitute for many slower, older, and more expensive ways to keep in touch: the holiday card, the change-of-address notice, the birth announcement, the alumni notes page, the vacation slideshow, and so on. It also provided a way to keep track of someone you didn't think you wanted to see, just in case you changed your mind. Twitter made it polite and easy to communicate with people you don't even know. While these different forms serve many purposes, not all of them useful, the progression from one to the next increased users' ability to maintain, quickly and cheaply, those weaker social connections that might fade away otherwise. They are all "contact aggregators," each one more efficient than the ones that came before.

But do they work? Do these digital solutions save time and improve our lives? The question reminds me of a story I've heard about an executive assistant in one of the top economics departments in the country back in the late 1980s. Highly competent and comfortable with her electric typewriter, she was wary when her department bought her, for the first time, a personal computer, a printer, and word processing software. As she tried out these time-saving, productivity-enhancing technologies, she grew frustrated. Everything that had been familiar was now new and different, and though she was good at her job, she fell behind in her work. Finally, one morning, frustrated again, she poured her mug of coffee into the vent in the back of her new computer, and when the destroyed machine was carted away, she went back to using her electric typewriter.

She wasn't wrong to question whether or not new technology would help her do her particular job better. Professor Paul David of Stanford, among others, has shown that technological innovations may not enhance productivity until the next generation of infrastructure is designed with them in mind. (Steam engines had belts that rotated vertically; steam-powered factories were designed to be tall and narrow, which limited the usefulness of electrical engines. Only when new, horizontal factories were built did the electric motor make a big impact on factory productivity.) Although in the long run that executive assistant's university and her nation saw a net gain in productivity as a result of personal computer technology, it was a slow and uneven process. There is no certainty that this particular executive assistant, doing her specific work, would have been better served by an early word processing program than by a top-of-the-line electric typewriter and copy machine.

In the same way, while the multimedia solutions to the overwhelm should, in the long run, save time and improve lives, there is no reason to think that this year's solutions are the right ones, or that every individual will be better served by new innovations. Current versions may yet prove to be transitional forms that are more trouble than they're worth, like the "Flash-matic" television that changed channels in response to sunlight through the window. That assistant was exercising her own judgment as a consumer of new media forms, and depending on how much longer she intended to keep her job and how quickly her department needed to computerize, her choice may have been, for her, efficient and wise.

If she made a mistake, perhaps it was to make her decision in isolation, alone with her frustration and her coffee mug—a bit like the writer Saul Bellow, struggling to process all the news in each day's newspaper by himself. I don't actually know if she consulted with her peers in the economics departments and with others in similar jobs to learn how best to adapt to the new machinery. I don't know how much she discovered about the advantages she might have enjoyed had she made it through the transition to word processing. But I do know that for individuals and businesses evaluating new media options today, the job of deciding what is or is not worthwhile will be overwhelming unless they find peers and curators to do some of the thinking for them. Wise businesses offer themselves as curators, providing the guidance that can be as valuable as the choices themselves.

4

THE FOURTH FACTOR

CONVERGENCE REMAKES COMMUNICATION—
AND ORGANIZATIONS

I knew the first time I saw *USA Today* that big changes were coming, and that I was going to have make sure that the *Washington Post*, where I was assistant managing editor and metro editor, could meet them. Until 1982, with the exception of the *Wall Street Journal* and, in a limited way, the *New York Times*, there had been only local general-interest newspapers; but *USA Today* sent its final edition by satellite to printers all over the country, enabling it to compete in all fifty states and beyond. Its most lasting innovations, though, were not in delivering the printed paper but in presenting content: new ways that news stories could be told, with groundbreaking use of color photographs and graphics.

Traditional newspapers presented a lot of text and a small number of black-and-white pictures, but *USA Today* relied heavily on visual aids such as color pictures, charts, and diagrams, as well as national polls that made public perceptions part of the story— elements that had not been a major part of written news to that point. I noticed that when I asked for more graphics and diagrams for our stories, the reporters would gripe—they were writers: they wanted to *write* the story. But while I was just as committed as they were to telling the story, I wasn't quite so committed to telling it *in words*. I was more concerned about telling it efficiently. If you could tell a story in less time, using whatever tools you had, you would do your reader a favor. My first successes in journalism had been taking and editing photographs; I could see that *USA Today* with its great use of visual aids and color photography was onto something. It quickly became the largest-circulation newspaper in the country. Their new storytelling methods were changing the entire business, with implications for any company with news to communicate about its products, its brands, and itself.

So, as an example of the cascade of convergences that keeps remaking our world, let me explain how the convergence of new storytelling methods played out in the newspaper business.

To understand the threat *USA Today* posed to my organization, I made a comparison of how the two papers handled the same material. I looked at a story about a report that came from the Department of Agriculture. In the *Post*, it was a twenty-inch story, one full column next to an advertisement. The story had a small headline that did nothing to draw you in. It was an excellent, well-crafted piece, but you had to be interested in the Department of Agriculture to spend the full ten minutes it would take to read, which meant that at least 90 percent of our readers didn't read it. (We knew that readers spent an average of thirty minutes with the daily paper, no matter what was in it.) *USA Today* ran their story in only half the space, but it had a headline, a subheadline under that headline, a head shot of the Agriculture Department official who was quoted, a colorful graphic, and captions under both the photo and the graphic. Although they only used five inches of type, there were six graphic "touch points" you could absorb in less than fifteen seconds. To me, the question was: whose reader was better off? Was it the reader offered the detailed, well-crafted story who probably skipped most of it, or the reader offered a less-detailed, more conveniently presented story?

The convergence in storytelling technology led to a more basic and powerful question: *what business were we in?* To me, the answer was clear. We were not in the business of creating a deep and correct factual record that most people would ignore; our job was to inform people—to get the story across. So I kept pushing my writers to go with the graphic tools, not because I didn't value a great story but because it seemed clear that when you have a choice of how to convey that story, you should explore which of those methods is most compelling and effective *for the reader.* I can't tell you, for instance, how many times I was able to cut four or five inches from a story by replacing a description of the location of a crime or other event with a small map.

Of course, news sources that have moved online don't have to choose between giving you graphics and giving you the full text—in the virtual world, there is endless space for both. Those readers who prefer the more detailed version of a story can click on links to access more detail and analysis. Yet now that any message can be delivered by text, images, audio, and video, or all of the above, which combination is best? When a picture is worth a thousand words, whether in a news article or a textbook or even a novel, wouldn't a good multimedia "writer" or "editor" cut the words and use the picture? If a video conveys a setting or an idea more graphically, why not use the video? That's the idea behind the Vook, the video-novel hybrid that has partnered with Anne Rice, for example, to offer vampire stories that include video of the setting and key plot points.

And when it comes to news and information, what about mobile graphics, interactive graphics, a soundtrack, hypertext links to definitions, spot quizzes, and educational games, not to mention updates of changes in real time? We already have the technology to create a "magical" digital newspaper, like the one in the world of *Harry Potter,* with pictures that move and interviewees who speak to the reader. Would that convergence be an improvement?

We don't know yet. So far, for the most part, different media forms on websites remain segregated in separate "silos." News or entertainment sites can link you to a video; National Public Radio can offer the choice of listening to their stories or reading them; but few creators and editors are fluent in all of the technological choices for storytelling. Just as a great news editor in the past developed a feel for when to run a photo and when to use a quote, the great multimedia editors of the future will direct us to video and audio and animation and back again, conducting the different sections of their newsgathering "orchestra," or perhaps acting more like a producer in a recording studio.

No one knows yet what further combinations and inventions are possible, but they are not far off. Consider the mystery novel. If I'm reading it on my smartphone or iPad, why can't the publisher sync a musical soundtrack with the turning of the pages? When the detective encounters a piece of evidence, why shouldn't I see the murder weapon in a photograph? Perhaps I could be enabled to zoom in on the photograph, filter the picture in different ways using photo software, and, in general, participate in the examination of a crime scene while an ominous soundtrack plays in the background? If, based on my own examination of the evidence, I can change the outcome of the story, would that be an inferior experience of the novel or an improvement? Would I still be "reading a mystery novel?" Would I be "playing a multimedia game?" Or is this a new form altogether?

Along the same lines, what if a clothing designer could send a life-size hologram of herself to your home to talk you through her new line, explaining the rationale for the latest designs—the new season's "story"—while you looked at full-size holograms of the clothes? What if you could then create a hologram of yourself, matching your measurements, so you could "dress yourself" in virtual versions of the clothes and see how you would look in them from someone else's perspective? I can't say whether we would consider that a new kind of home shopping program, a form of fashion journalism, or a 3D multimedia website. What I would need to know, if I worked in the fashion business, is whether consumers preferred this convergence of sales call, advertisement, and editorial content to traditional in-store shopping. And if they preferred it, how would companies have to reorganize themselves to meet that preference?

Some new forms of communication announce themselves with striking new technology, such as a virtual-reality bodysuit. Others arrive almost unnoticed. When novelist Norman Mailer called HBO's television show *The Sopranos* not just a great show but "the closest thing to the Great American Novel in our culture today," and several other high-profile novelists agreed, he raised a bigger question: has the novel met its match? Is it possible that serialized, advertisement-free television, unconstrained by the content restrictions the federal government imposes on broadcast networks, available to viewers who (like novel readers) can take in the story over time and at their own pace, has "out-noveled" the novel? For years, there have been many predictions that new media would one day lead to new literary forms, just as the printing press did in its time. Perhaps that has happened already. Does that mean there will be fewer novels and more television dramas? Or does it mean that there is a new way for television to build readership for the novel? The revolution in storytelling created by convergence is already well under way. Witness the rapid success of the iPad.

CONSUMERS CONVERGE WITH PRODUCERS

Some of these new forms are rising because technology lets consumers help create the content they want. At one end of the spectrum is a show like *American Idol*. At the other end is *Star Trek: New Voyages*, a series of fan webisodes that appeared in 2007, two years after Paramount canceled its one remaining *Star Trek* TV series and before development of a new series of movies. At the moment the industry thought the Star Trek franchise was best left fallow, these fans surprised Hollywood with a new series that won *TV Guide*'s 2007 Online Video Award for best sci-fi webisode.

Created by amateurs in their spare time and on a small budget, and defeating better-funded competitors, *New Voyages* featured a ship and crew similar to that of the original *Star Trek* series from the 1960s. Its soundtrack and special effects—spaceships in flight, interstellar vistas, phaser battles—were comparable to that show's as well. The main cast and the director were amateurs, but a number of professional actors who had appeared in the *Star Trek* series and movies also appeared on the web show as guest stars. The results were impressively close to that of the original series, suggesting just how much could be accomplished outside professional television studios.

At the time, this unexpected amateur triumph prompted a fair amount of talk in the film and television industry, mostly from those insisting that amateur television could not compete with professional products. Robert Thompson of Syracuse University's Center for Television and Popular Culture called the Internet "one great big farm team" for mainstream media, a source of their future talent. But while traditional television will harvest talent from amateur efforts on the web, and while professional television networks will always have an edge in terms of production values, that may not settle the question of whether the amateurs could, in many instances, take over. I suspect it will only be a matter of time before the technological disadvantages of amateur television—the imperfect production, the echoes of TV technology from an earlier time, the lack of cutting-edge special effects—become, in the hands of some innovative amateur, the new signs of authenticity or marks of rebellion, making the high-tech perfection of network television seem, by comparison, artificial and out of touch.

To focus on who will "win," amateur or professional, is to miss the central point about convergence: the new doesn't replace the old; the new and the old combine. Businesses have discovered that consumers often prefer amateur advertisements to the ones made by Madison Avenue firms. Lego, whose growth in recent years has come from kits that allow the buyer to build complex models created by Lego designers (such as spaceships from *Star Wars* or figures from the *Bionicles* science fantasy world), also invites fans to design their own models. They can post pictures to the Lego site and even order custom sets of Lego pieces that include a step-by-step guide for assembling their model and a box with an illustration of the model on the cover. Examples of designs posted on the site that are unlike the usual Lego fare include a violin, a dead soldier, and an Arabian-style observatory tower for studying the heavens. Lego has crowdsourced toy design.

At present, most amateur talent remains mainly confined to its "silos," just as nontraditional media—video on newspaper or magazine websites, video games in relation to movies, and so on—are confined to theirs. But as innovators continue to find ways to release these elements and sources from their usual confines, convergence will become the long-term engine of the media transition. Within media companies, there is already a pressing need for more employees with hybrid talents: people who combine the traditional skills of creating and editing, and of maintaining a connection to an audience, with the new media skills required by multimedia technologies. When the Center for Investigative Reporting in Berkeley teamed up recently with public radio station KQED to distribute a story about nitrate poisoning of water sources, they quickly realized that they needed to send the print, radio, and video reporters out together and then figure out which parts of the story should be told through which media. In time they produced three radio stories, two print stories, a video documentary, and background context on the web to hold them all together. The combination of financial and creative pressures is requiring more and more of these convergent collaborations.

Within non-media companies, there is growing awareness of the need to understand the new media platforms, but that is only the beginning. Many platforms that seem important today will likely be replaced in a few years, because this fourth factor, the ongoing convergence of technologies, media forms, and aspects of our lives, will continue to intensify the other three.

If my Vook or my (imaginary) interactive, multimedia mystery novel is halfway between a traditional novel and a video game, how will my feelings about novels or video games change?

And as the media platforms converge, so do the businesses that use them. A traditional newspaper office handled just a few different jobs—writing, editing, photography, subscriptions, and sales. Printing was handled separately at a printing press. Delivery was handled by truckers, again separately. Newsstand sales were again handled separately. Not only were the different forms of storytelling walled off from each other, but so were different aspects of the overall business. Then the walls separating the different aspects of the business fell. It was possible for one organization to "print" their own newspaper, "deliver" that (paperless) newspaper, sell that newspaper, and update and redistribute that content in countless ways. Not only newspaper customers but the newspaper business experienced an explosion of choice: they could publish a limitless number of "editions" and offer their content on an increasingly complex variety of different platforms. They could also price what they sold in a variety of different ways—and as they soon discovered, they would have to if they wanted to survive. Those in the business began searching for new strategic curators, to help them decide what to do with this new freedom. What had begun as a change in storytelling transformed the entire industry, and those transformations continue.

This era of convergence, which has already lasted fifteen years, will not end soon. While the technological shift to digital media is becoming familiar, the ongoing reinvention of storytelling is just getting under way. No new technology or new form of media, no matter how much attention it's getting today, will necessarily last any longer than dial-up Internet or the eight-track tape. There can be no permanent solutions to the challenges of the C-scape, because there is no one permanent C-scape. To succeed in this time of ongoing and accelerating change, businesses and consumers alike need new habits of thought, to grasp the new forms, threats, and opportunities of our changed world.

PART TWO

WHAT HAPPENS TO MARKETS?

5

MARKETING BEYOND THE PURCHASE FUNNEL

ADVERTISING BECOMES "CONTENT"

In the summer of 2008, CEO Bob Rosenschein and his fast-growing informational website Answers.com faced a turning point. Already one of the top websites, with 24 million unique users a month, and flush with a new cash infusion from the venture capital firm Redpoint Ventures, Answers.com was now trying to become profitable. In the past, its main source of revenue for the site had been text ads provided by Google AdSense: if you went to the site and typed in the question, "What are Siamese cats?" you would see a short list of sponsored links above the search results. These sponsored links might include a pet health website, cat breeders, and similar topics of concerns to Siamese cat owners. They had none of the traditional qualities that made advertisements attract eyeballs—no images, no video, nothing but simple lines of text, yet they were the main source of revenue for the site.

A year earlier, in 2007, Answers.com had made the decision to hire a sales force to sell display ads, such as web banners, with animated or static images, audio, and interactive elements. This choice seemed forward-thinking, as it allowed for the convergence of text, audio, video, and interactivity to create more technologically sophisticated messaging on the site. Yet it didn't work. Once the new display ads went up, overall revenue went down. The banners were distracting customers from reading text ads but were not generating enough of their own revenue to make up the difference and pay for the new advertising sales force.

What to do? Management came up with a radical solution: close the new display advertising department, send the new employees home, and run only text ads, optimized with better placement on the page and more attractive use of colors and fonts. That stunning decision to abandon traditional advertising turned the company around. Revenue increased, the company eliminated costs, and Answers.com, an ad-driven website without either a conventional advertising department or any relationship with an advertising agency, began to turn a profit.

One of the most famous quotations in all of marketing is attributed to John Wanamaker, the pioneer department store merchant: "Half the money I spend on advertising is wasted; the trouble is, I don't know which half." That quote gives a feel for the old-media model of advertising: imprecise, unpredictable, but comfortably so. No one ever knew exactly which ads got to which customers, but everyone seemed to agree that if you exposed a captive audience to the same message frequently enough, eventually you'd get through. But in the C-scape, it's as if John Wanamaker could finally learn what's not worth his money. According to research from Veronis Suhler Stevenson, in 2005 companies spent on average 38 percent of their marketing budgets on advertising. By 2015, that number is expected to be cut in half. "From the standpoint of the powers that be on Madison Avenue," says Jeffrey Rayport, a consultant and former Harvard Business School professor, "it's the decline and fall of the Roman Empire."

THE PURCHASE FUNNEL CRACKS

Why have the old models have become less effective? How do you replace them? Let's start with the old advertising methods, and why they don't lead to sales the way they used to. Would you like to stop reading right now and view some sponsored messages? Probably not. While some ads, such as those introduced each year during the Super Bowl broadcast, are enjoyable the first few times, we rarely *hope* to see one. Audiences have generally tried to tune them out, and advertisers have countered by trying to force the message through with repetition, not just in conventional advertisements but in editorial content (often placed by public relations firms) and in the training of store clerks.

The traditional model was known as the "purchase funnel" because some of the potential customers who were exposed to ads "funneled down" from simple awareness (there are new models of televisions for sale) to more meaningful familiarity with a brand and its features (they have high-definition 1080i screens with a contrast ratio of a million to one), and then to consideration of how the products would match their particular desires (a picture so clear you feel as if you're actually there). Finally, after repeated exposure to the messages of this media monopoly, some consumers made a purchase.

In the C-scape, however, while a potential TV buyer may still become aware of new models through advertisements, when he wonders how much these new features are worth to him, he has a vast new world of sources to consult. Let's call him John. Perhaps John posts a question online—"How much difference do these new screen features make?"—and a friend or even a stranger answers with a link to a column by David Pogue, tech reviewer for the *New York Times*. John might never have heard of Pogue, but now in seconds he reads the following: "Day in and day out, the electronics industry manipulates us. They publish 'speeds and feeds' in big bold type—measurements that turn out to mean almost nothing." Pogue quickly demolishes some of the most-repeated marketing claims in electronics: that the number of megapixels predicts the quality of a camera, that computer processor speed makes any difference to typical users, and so on until he gets to televisions, "Don't get me started about the ridiculous TV-specification benchmarks. Do you really think the average person could see the difference between 720p and 1080i? Or between a contrast ratio of 500,000:1 versus a million to 1?"

John, now only three or four minutes into his research into TV features, has broken the television industry's traditional-media monopoly on information—that is, he has cracked the purchase funnel. He is free to seek out like-minded experts and peers who can address his concerns. In place of the authority of traditional media, he can substitute alternative media he selects himself. Instead of accepting the facts he's given, he can do his own research, outstripping the knowledge that any given salesclerk has about any one particular product. (As former Home Depot chief marketing officer John Ross observed, "Consumers themselves are transforming. [They] walk into a retail location knowing more about the products than the retail associates.") He picks his own curators—and changes them as often as he likes.

If he does go to an electronics retailer, a salesclerk may still tell him, as the clerk is trained to do, that a million-to-one contrast ratio will "future proof" his purchase, but he'll be armed with his own personalized information that backs up his individual experience: when he looks at the more expensive screen, he can't see a difference. Meanwhile, he will have found support for the differences that do matter to him. Maybe his concerns are environmental, and he wants a television with a small carbon footprint and recyclable parts. He may well leave with a very different television than the one his neighbor will buy, despite their demographic similarities.

CAN'T MARKETERS FIGHT BACK?

In the C-scape, faced with these changes, marketers have only two alternatives. One is to try to force consumers back into the funnel. Some of the power to compel an audience lost to technological innovations can be regained, at least for a while, either with new innovations or by blocking existing ones. In the 1990s, for example, Panasonic and some other VCR makers began marketing a videocassette recorder that sensed the beginning of a television advertisement during playback and automatically fast-forwarded through it. Popular among viewers who wanted to skip ads—it shifted the balance of laziness back in their favor—it was quietly removed from the market, and advertisers enjoyed several more years of captive television audiences. Now, although the digital video recorder is here to stay, there are situations in which skipping of ads is not permitted. Often, before you watch a video or read an article online, you have to take in a commercial message—many online providers of television reruns take this approach. By enforcing some of the old viewing requirements with new technologies, advertisers can preserve some of their old business model for themselves and their sponsors.

But a digital-technology arms race in which advertisers fight consumers to force them back into their old dependent position will never win back all of the attention that advertisements used to command. And some attempts to do so will likely spark a backlash such as the one that afflicted the music industry. So while some of these approaches—the ones that don't insult and provoke the consumer—are worth pursuing, they will never recapture the old attention monopoly.

The second alternative is to accept consumers' new powers of choice and find ways to profit by helping them use their new freedom. Most companies today are attempting a shortcut version of that second choice. They have identified new technologies or approaches that they lack. They hope that by adding a few new-media initiatives to what they already do, they can patch the holes in the broken purchase funnel, rebuild their near-monopoly on messaging, and reassert their old authority over the consumer. But for most companies, these attempts only perpetuate their outdated strategy. Journalist Mark Coatney's criticism of the magazine industry applies increasingly across all of business: "They all too often latch on to new technology (Let's make an iPhone app! Let's build a Facebook fan page! Let's create print ads with RFID scan technology! Let's start a Tumblr blog!) without understanding the *reason* behind that beautiful technology. It's not a strategy; it's a last gasp tactic."

Similarly, I hear a lot of bold and overstated declarations about new directions in marketing: "The brand belongs to the customer," for example. It sounds like a strong, fresh approach to marketing. Unfortunately, it's not true. Customers don't create brands. They don't maintain brands, and they don't much care if a company profits from them or not. Only companies do those things. Saying "the brand belongs to the customer" is a way of flattering consumers, acknowledging their new power of choice while trying to figure out how to deal with them. It's stalling for time.

Technology damaged the purchase funnel, but the resulting

challenge for business is not simply a question of technology, it's a question of customer relationships. I thought of the ever-increasing difficulty of those relationships when I heard the sad tale of Drew Barrymore's character in *He's Just Not That into You*, a movie about the difficulties of contemporary dating. She has met a guy who she thinks she likes, but she finds it unexpectedly challenging even to contact him so he can begin to get to know her. She says:

> *I had this guy leave me a voice mail at work, so I called him at home. Then he emailed me to my Blackberry so I texted to his cell—and now you just have to go around checking all these different portals just to get rejected by seven different technologies. It's exhausting!*

Although she has mastered the many new technologies by which the man in question prefers to communicate, the technologies by themselves do her little good because she can't inspire him to give her a chance. Like the no-longer-captive audience for advertisements, he sees her communications coming and limits her level of permission to contact him—she tries to phone him at home, but he limits her to an email. She texts his cell, but he doesn't respond. She works harder to reach him but gets less of his attention. What she needs, just like a business that relies on advertising, is not just to master the new technologies of communication but to understand how to use them to move the person on the other end to *want* to receive and participate in that communication.

THE NEW PRIVACY

The Internet, smartphones, and other new forms of communication are conventionally described as agents of informality that break down barriers to communication; but they have also re-formalized our lives and put up new barriers to marketing messages. Two generations ago, a telephone call carried a certain weight of obligation, almost like a visitor banging on your door. But increasingly we live in a complex new culture of layered permissions and partial grants of attention. We use technologies not just as our butler but as our receptionist and our bouncer, to limit and control others' access to us. My father will answer a call from a stranger during dinner; my daughter doesn't always answer a call from someone she knows, no matter what the time. And increasingly, when I reach someone on the phone, I'm aware that the other person may have granted me only partial attention, saving the rest for composing a message or keeping an eye on a video screen while we talk.

These new levels of permission may trump old social conventions—at Broadway shows now, a pre-curtain announcement pleads with the audience not to text during the performance, a plea that someone usually ignores. At the same time, direct mail solicitations, which were always the most profitable source of fundraising for nonprofits, are expected to die along with the generation that still opens all their mail. Email open rates continue to fall. The government offers www.donotcall.gov, a website that will remove your name from telemarketers' lists, and Catalog Choice, a free, nonprofit service, will contact catalog providers and tell them to stop sending to you. Unless you have personal approval from the recipient—and how many ads get your personal approval?— it's getting harder and harder to get through.

WHO WANTS ADS?

I believe the future of advertising depends on changing its most basic assumptions. First, rather than insisting on advertising as a forced and unpleasant interruption, advertisers need to make consumers *want* to give their attention to ads. Is that possible? On first hearing it sounds . . . unlikely. Yet researchers at the NYU Stern School of Business asked their test subjects to watch an episode of a sitcom, some watching with and some without commercials, and to rate their enjoyment at intervals along the way. They found that those who watched with commercials rated it higher—and that this was true even among subjects who had reported on an earlier questionnaire that they preferred to avoid advertisements. This result seemed to confirm the psychological principle that the pleasure of any positive experience declines through repetition and over time—the tenth bite in a row of even your favorite food is less pleasurable than the first. Yet taking a break can refresh that pleasure, just as a sip of a drink can clear the palate and make food more enjoyable again.

Of course, many factors will make a difference here: what you think of the ads you are shown, how often you've seen them before, and whether your show was crafted around these breaks, to heighten suspense, perhaps, or to provide a rest after a crescendo of jokes. Sometimes an irritating advertisement can make the show seem better by contrast. But for me, the study helped underline a key idea: past assumptions we have about advertising don't hold up, sometimes for worse but also for better.

I found practical confirmation of this idea after Nielsen changed the way it measured television ratings to account for DVR systems. Over the objections of the networks, they replaced traditional program ratings with what they called "live plus three" ratings, measuring viewing for the commercials in shows watched either live or played back on digital video recorders within three days. Most people in the industry expected disaster—that viewers would skip all ads, ratings for ads would plummet, and sponsors would lose their motivation to buy advertising. Instead, when Nielsen measured the actual behavior of viewers, DVR by DVR, they found that nearly half of the ads were still getting watched. As Andy Donchin, director of media investment for the ad agency Carat said, "The DVR was going to kill television. It hasn't." And there were surprise benefits for shows with relatively small "live" audiences that turned out to have unexpected popularity among delayed watchers. Shows slated for cancellation due to apparently low ratings won new lives. Some saw ratings increases of 20 percent when the delayed viewers were included. And live shows, such as Jay Leno's, which had bragged about being DVR-proof, suffered in comparison.

Explanations were offered from all directions. Some analysts saw a persistence of an old habit, despite the new technological options: maybe people kept watching commercials because they always had and they forgot, in the moment, that they had a choice. Some ad agencies took credit, claiming that it was the result of new and better ads. Some pointed to the balance of laziness: it's easier sometimes for a viewer just to keep watching, rather than find the remote and push the fast-forward button. To me, the point is not to argue about the precise psychology, but to observe that while far fewer television ads are being watched than in the past (50 percent among the DVR users rather than over 90 percent among viewers of live television, according to Nielsen estimates), it is clear that many viewers will still watch ads *even when they have the technical ability to skip them.* So we need to ask: if commercial interruptions have even the potential to be welcome breaks rather than hostile intrusions, what changes might make an audience welcome them more?

I see three opportunities. Each offers the target audience something desirable—something entertaining, valuable or useful, or a combination.

1. Offer consumers payment for their time and attention with some form of tangible reward. On the Modelinia website, for example, the models not only wear the advertised makeup and beauty products, they also demonstrate step-by-step techniques for applying them.

2. Converge ads with entertainment content. When the product is part of the story or the event, as in a product placement, the pleasure of the entertainment can't be unscrambled from the commercial message.

3. Provide useful consumer information. Walgreens, for example, caters to eco-conscious consumers of its health and beauty aids by providing extensive information about products' ingredients on its website.

PAY CONSUMERS FOR THEIR ATTENTION

This new idea is in fact very old. The mass media always offered ads as a form of barter: if you pay attention to our ads, they promised, we'll give you content in exchange. Look at our print ads, and we'll give you the articles below cost because your subscription will be subsidized by ad revenue. Watch the commercials on television, and we'll give you the shows for free. But now the bargain has broken down. So one response is to sweeten the deal. When Microsoft created a variety show, the *bing-a-thon* to advertise its new Bing search engine, it broadcast it on Hulu.com, the online video service supported by commercials. But viewers of the *bing-a-thon* were offered payment in the form of uninterrupted viewing in the future: if they watched the Bing program, they could watch other television shows on Hulu.com without ads.

Websites such as Groupon and Woot take another approach to

paying visitors to look at advertising. By offering one product or service each day at a high discount—from 50 to 90 percent—they compensate members for checking their offerings each day. The promise of the bargain makes the ads—and therefore the entire website—worth careful attention.

CONVERGE ADVERTISING WITH ENTERTAINMENT

The second possibility is for advertisers to create content that is blended with advertising. That way, instead of interrupting the enjoyable show for the unpleasant but fiscally necessary commercial message, the two mix together, and a spoonful of sugar helps the medicine go down. Convergence of advertising and entertainment was central to television's past, when companies such as General Electric would hire advertising agencies to produce television programs in which the host and stars of the show would also read advertisements and public relations messages on the part of the company. In 1954, the *General Electric Theater*, hosted by actor and future president Ronald Reagan, and featuring adaptations of popular plays, fiction, and movies with stars such as Jack Benny, Alan Ladd, and Joan Crawford, became the country's number one weekly dramatic program.

Mixed in with the anthology of dramatic pieces were other programming elements that marketed the GE brand directly and indirectly. Don Herbert, well known to TV audiences for his role in *Watch Mr. Wizard*, was cast as the "General Electric Progress Reporter," bringing the audience news about the latest electric devices. One telecast featured Jimmy Stewart celebrating the first anniversary of the electric utility's "Live Better Electrically" campaign and "National Electric Week." The closing commercial featured Nancy and Ronald Reagan in the kitchen of a Total Electric home. "When you live better electrically," Reagan told viewers, "you lead a richer, fuller, more satisfying life. And it's something all of us in this modern age can have."

Later, when it became possible to sell twenty or more ads for a single show, networks did not want to limit themselves to a single main sponsor. They also didn't want to be associated with one main sponsor whose brand might overshadow that of the show. But in the era of the digital video recorder, if a TV show has twenty-five ads and a company buys only one of them, there's a high probability that that ad will be skipped. Sponsorship is appealing again because it's hard to miss, even when the viewer holds a remote.

Such an approach caught on early in sports broadcasts, where different aspects of the show (the introduction of the players by name, the instant replay, the daily trivia question) are identified with different sponsors, whose logos and taglines the announcers repeat—the "Target play of the day" and so forth. National Public Radio does this effectively as well. Similarly, on reality programs the sponsors' products are likely to show up in the contestants' hands—a *Survivor* character receiving a gift box may well be handed a box decorated with a store logo.

We can expect to see more of the same in all kinds of entertainment. Let's go back to the *bing-a-thon*. Fifty years after the *General Electric Theater*, this hybrid of a telethon, a game show, and an infomercial was hosted by comic actor Fred Willard, along with comedians from *Saturday Night Live* and *Attack of the Show*, as well as vibraphonist Roy Ayers, who performed his song "Searching" to underline the search-engine theme. A far cry in tone from GE's earnest promises of "a richer, fuller, more satisfying life" through electrical appliances, the *bing-a-thon* tried to establish its brand as hip and youthful through absurdist comedy: in one sketch, Fred Willard competed with a professional cat groomer to see how many

Bing searches he could perform online before the groomer finished trimming his cat. ("This is the best thing that's happened to me since I put Mom away in a home," Mr. Willard quipped.) Yet despite the drastic difference in style and tone, and also in broadcast technology, the underlying attempt was the same: to make an advertising message appealing by weaving it into the entertainment.

We will continue to see more convergences of this kind, as well as more attempts to insert advertising into existing programming. Not only does it make the advertising messages impossible to speed through or remove, it has the possibility of lending the excitement and cachet of the content to the advertised product. And while this point may seem obvious, sometimes the method is subtle, even sneaky, and intentionally so.

It was not widely known, for example, until the third season of AMC's hit *Mad Men*, a drama about a fictional 1960s advertising agency, that the show not only referred to 1960s brands as part of its period storyline, but also contained product placements negotiated by still-extant brands. These included London Fog coats and Stolichnaya vodka. The endorsements by characters were sometimes explicit: in one scene, agency head Roger Sterling (played by John Slattery) not only names the brand of vodka he chooses, he also denies it to an out-of-favor junior account agent, saying, "Not the Stoli!" Yet both the show's producers and the representatives played down the use of product placements. A representative for London Fog told Brandweek.com that the company's PR agency had facilitated the brand's placement, yet wouldn't reveal what compensation the show received. Andrey Skurikhin, a partner at SPI Group, which owns the Stoli brand, stated that he *didn't* pay for placement. And the AMC network's president and general manager, Charlie Collier, refused to provide any information to Brandweek about advertisements built into the show. "We absolutely have product integration on the show," he explained, "but you shouldn't know which ones are paid and which ones aren't."

Why shouldn't we know? For the same reason that advertisers find these types of product placements increasingly necessary. When a viewer is aware that a product placement is an ad, that awareness interrupts, and possibly diminishes, the realism of the show. The success of this form of convergence depends in part on preventing viewers from thinking about the mechanics of commerce. In the *Mad Men* placements, not only did advertising converge with entertainment, but the real-life representatives of both the sponsors and the television network had to collude to hide where one ended and the other began, not just in the show but in their public statements. For the convergence to succeed fully, the actual company representatives had to play a supporting role to the televised drama: even executives of media companies are finding that the convergences of sales and entertainment are drawing them deeper into media.

Compare the *Mad Men* placements to websites with viral appeal, such as "Subservient Chicken." On this site, the user encounters what appears to be a webcam showing a person in a chicken suit, awaiting instructions. The "chicken" performs actions the user requests, anything from yoga to falling down dead to a Michael Jackson–style moonwalk, over one hundred separate commands, with some exceptions. Told to do something he finds offensive, the "chicken" waves a scolding finger. Told to eat McDonald's food, he makes a gagging motion. Not in fact a true live webcam, but rather a collection of pre-recorded video clips, the site is an interactive game in which the object is to figure out what the chicken will do and why. He is demonstrating that at Burger King, you can "get chicken just the way you like it." The Burger King logo and copyright line are small; the link to their website marked simply

"BK Tendercrisp." Like *Mad Men*, the site attracts an audience by offering entertainment; the hope is that users' feelings will spread from the entertainment to the sponsoring brand.

WHAT HAPPENS TO CONTENT?

These various convergences of commercial messages with creative content have clear benefits for the sponsor, but what happens to the content itself? Common wisdom holds that when it comes to entertainment, it doesn't matter if it's blended in with commercial messages, no more than the playing of a ball game changes if the name of the stadium changes. (In my hometown of San Francisco, the names of both stadiums have changed repeatedly, from Candlestick Park to 3Com Park to Monster Park and back to Candlestick Park again, and in only one decade the new ballpark changed from PacBell Park to SBC Park to AT&T Park.) But this is a gray area—while it may not destroy James Bond to drive a Chevy instead of his famous Aston Martin, at some point he seems less like the greatest spy in the world and more like any other spokesperson pitching the new model line of cars. The pressure to blend commercial message and creative content creates an ongoing tension.

ADVERTISING THAT CONVERGES WITH NEWS AND INFORMATION

There are more serious effects when the content being blended with sponsored messages also aspires to take on serious issues. Consider the Total Electricity Home that General Electric built for Ronald and Nancy Reagan and featured on the *General Electric Theater*. It was packed with so many electrical appliances that it overwhelmed the building's original wiring; the company had to install a 3,000-

pound steel cabinet outside their home for their fuse box. With a sponsor so committed to maximizing the use of electrical appliances, it's hard to imagine how the *General Electric Theater* could have done justice to programming that explored, for example, the dangers of nuclear energy. On the other hand, some writers have managed to strike a balance between the needs of their sponsors and the needs of their stories: *Mad Men* not only features successful, attractive men drinking premium liquor morning, noon, and night, it also shows lives wrecked by alcoholism.

But if the convergence of advertising and entertainment has been judged to create tolerable challenges to artistic integrity, the convergence of advertising and news has often been viewed as poison. News organizations have traditionally gone to extraordinary lengths to protect journalistic integrity from the influence of commercial messages. At most newspapers, advertising representatives were forbidden to walk through the news room. This practice was one of many used to erect a "Chinese wall" between advertising and the creation of news content. This same separation was observed in the printed newspaper itself, where articles were grouped into topical sections, each one supported by advertisements, but the ads were kept separate from related stories. (You weren't supposed to see an article about corruption in a certain brokerage house, for example, positioned next to an advertisement for that broker's competitor.) As Tony Burman, ex–editor in chief of CBC News, famously said, "Every news organization has only its credibility and reputation to rely on." That meant keeping the news content separate from its sponsorship.

But in the C-scape, digital technology has toppled the old Chinese wall. The biggest factor is Internet search itself. If you search for the name of an airline, your results will jumble news and commercial messages together. This powerful and, I think, irresistible convergence of information and commercial is the only form of advertisement for which revenue rose in the recession of 2008. It is what Answers.com embraced when it folded its traditional advertising department and gave all its space to Google AdSense. The approach is effective because it does two things at once, first of all targeting its audience according to the interests they express in their Internet searches and second, as David Jackson, CEO of the financial news site Seeking Alpha, put it, doing so when the audience is in a "transactional mind-set," seeking new information and new products. It targets the people who want certain information at the moment they want it, and by doing so, it gets far better results than forced repetition.

ADVERTISING IS NOW CONTENT

The lesson here is not that search-based AdSense is better than traditional display advertising for driving sales—often it is, sometimes it isn't, as the following chapters will show. Advertising can still create awareness and spark consideration of a product or a brand, but only if it provides content valuable to the consumer. The methods of advertising must change. In the past, advertising was a separate business from other media, set apart by its special power to force consumers to pay attention. Now advertising must get out of the monopolizing-attention business and join the rest of media, traditional and new, in the content business.

That shift has implications for the short and the long term. Right away, businesses need to realize that their idea of what makes for a great advertisement may be out of date. I still hear senior sales and marketing executives impressed with the latest technologies to force consumers to pay attention. When they buy online advertising, they favor "pre-roll" ads you have to watch before you get to see the video you want to see. They like rich media ads that "crawl" all over the computer screen, demanding to be read. They measure the success of their campaigns in click-throughs to their website. But all of these approaches only interrupt the user. If I'm on a certain website, I'm there because I want to be. Even if someone offers me interesting information—let's say the specs on a new car model I've been waiting to hear about—I'd much rather be able to mouse over and get the information without leaving the site, so I don't have to navigate back later to find my place again when I'm done. I'll give more attention to an ad, not less, if I'm not required to click through to another site.

Similarly, many in business are impressed with online video advertising because it is more sophisticated technologically than text, still images, or even mobile graphics. But the question they should be asking themselves is not a technology question, it's a storytelling question: Is video the best way to tell a story about the product that the viewer will want? Or is it only a rude interruption that ties up bandwidth and makes noise?

If you have a movie to sell, then yes, a movie trailer is often the best way to advertise it, because a trailer is a free sample of the movie. But for many products, being made to sit through video is uninformative and annoying. As Jackson of Seeking Alpha told me, quoting a colleague who did not want to be identified, "The senior manager of probably the largest owner of online financial video put it this way: 'Our readers do not want to watch videos of white men talking.'"

When video does seem the best storytelling choice for an ad, the goal should be to present it to viewers in a way that addresses the four C's. Offer consumers a choice of ads so they can select content that is worthwhile to them. Position the sponsor as a curator offering valuable options, rather than an authority imposing unpleasant demands on their time. One promising example is the Ad Selector, developed by Hulu. When viewers were offered a choice of ads by different brands to watch before the start of a movie or a television program, rather than being forced to watch one mandatory "pre-roll" ad, their recall scores were almost 300 percent higher than those given no choice. They paid better attention to ads they wanted to see. For that reason, "wanted" ads are more valuable, and in time the market should adjust to a world of fewer but more effective advertisements.

THE END OF MARKET SEGMENTATION?

But the implications of this profound change in advertising go far beyond the choice of particular advertising techniques. Companies must give up another of marketing's biggest assumptions: that they can segment consumers effectively based on traditional demographic categories such as age, sex, and income. Jean-Christophe Bedos, president of Boucheron, the French maker of jewelry and watches, describes the change in his industry this way: "The more we try to segment the market, the more we fail. People are increasingly individualists. They escape any categorizing. . . . It's very exciting, because our models are wrong."

Exciting it may be, but what is a marketer manager supposed to do? How can he or she design marketing messages and determine which ones to send to which consumers if the consumer base can't be segmented? After all, there can be only so many messages prepared about any given product, only so many consumer "interests" a company can serve. No company can say everything to everyone. "The end of market segmentation" can sound like another of those striking, yet impractical, slogans like "the customer owns the brand" or "content wants to be free." No matter how often such slogans are repeated, there will still be branded content from corporations. So how do you market without segmentation? Like any slogan, "the end of market segmentation" is a dangerous oversimplification. There will always be market segmentation. What has changed is *how* you identify the different slices of your market, and *who controls* the process for doing so. The underlying shift is due to the consumer's increased power—including the power to remain unpredictable.

THE MARKET IS THE RELATIONSHIP

"Marketing" used to involve a physical trip, a change of scene. You had to go to market to see what consumers needed and what they were buying. But as you make your way through the C-scape, the market is not necessarily a place anymore. Shopping happens wherever a consumer chooses to power up a laptop or a phone. Handheld technologies even make it possible now for someone to stand inside the physical walls of your competitor's business and complete a transaction with you. Where is the market now? In the relationship with the consumer, helping him or her to find what is compelling: "What specific model would suit me best? How would I use it? What more information do I need? What would make this experience more satisfying?" The goal is to become one of the sources the consumer trusts. He or she can go anywhere, digitally, and talk to almost anyone.

That is the reason most of the approaches to advertising I've suggested in this chapter don't sound much like advertising. Instead, they involve creating a good piece of entertainment, an informative article, a public relations campaign, or an innovative customer

6

TALK WITH, NOT AT

PUBLIC RELATIONS STILL
DELIVERS THE MESSAGE

Advertising has lost much of its power. Doesn't PR face the same fate? Distinguished from advertising because no money is exchanged for placement in media (at least we hope that's the case), PR was always advertising's kid brother, its younger, smaller, less-lucrative partner in messaging. It faces all the same challenges of the C-scape, yet unlike advertising, PR not only continues to thrive, but is raising its standing in the communications world. As Richard Edelman, president and chief executive officer of the Edelman public relations company, explains, PR is positioned to become "the lead discipline in the communications mix."

But if the endurance of PR is a crucial story of the C-scape, it's a story you might miss. During the recent economic downturn, this headline ran in *Crain's New York Business*: "PR Firms Can't Spin This News." The article explained that two-thirds of PR firms had seen declines that year, further evidence of a recession—not that anyone needed it. Yet that quick-snapshot statistic hid the real story: the average PR firm was outperforming advertising—for the first time ever. Data from Veronis Suhler Stevenson on future spending plans show a number of predictable trends—and one big surprise. The predictable trends were technological: big increases in spending on online media and mobile media; big decreases in spending on print ads and television ads. Yet the change for spending on PR was exactly where you wouldn't expect it.

Advertising agencies are offering more PR services: Saatchi & Saatchi, the global advertising firm, set up an advisory business in consumer social responsibility.

And across the full spectrum of business, the shift is clear. FedEx, whose pioneering ads were a highlight of the Super Bowl broadcast for eighteen years, shifted to a web-video campaign of slyly joking infomercials featuring the comedian Fred Willard. Instead of paying for expensive advertising slots at the Super Bowl, they were choosing to create a kind of FedEx comedy channel and hoping that potential customers would be drawn to them on You-Tube or FedEx's own website.

The FedEx example might lead you to believe the change is primarily technological: from traditional media to new—in this case, from television spots to Internet videos. The story was often reported: *FedEx is leaving TV for the web!* But focusing on the technological change, like focusing on the short-term effects of the economic downturn, was to miss the real story.

Like advertising, PR was until recently a creature of the traditional media. For many years, the term "public relations" was used interchangeably with "press relations" because the only real choice for reshaping your relationship with your public was through the intermediaries of the press and television. Yet as the changes of the C-scape hit, the underlying differences became clear.

THE RISE OF CONVERGENT PR

In the old days of PR, an agency would write a press release announcing whatever new development the client wanted known, have it typed and copied and stuffed in envelopes, and then mail them out to publications and other news organizations. Then the client would wait for those letters to be received, hoping for a front-page story or other prominent coverage a few days later. Traditional media's near-monopoly on communications meant that the editors and producers were the gatekeepers, deciding which press releases deserved coverage.

Then came the fax machine, which cut communication time from a few days to a few minutes. Soon the "blast fax" to multiple recipients lowered the cost of sending the same press release to large numbers of news outlets. While this speed didn't diminish the role of the press as gatekeepers, it gave those with a message to send an additional choice in where they could send it because cost was less of a constraint. Still, even as the Internet made communication nearly instantaneous, PR was still the same old game: get the press to cover you, because they are the only curators in town. The most successful people in PR were those who had good relationships with the gatekeepers and could negotiate special deals with them. Perhaps they would give one outlet an "exclusive," and allow them to break the news ahead of the press release being issued, in exchange for a promise that the story would get big play in the newspaper the next morning or on the news that night.

But in the C-scape, the top editorial blogs challenged traditional news outlets in reach and curatorial influence. In business news, TechCrunch, the tech blog that profiles start-ups, products, and websites, won over 3 million RSS feed subscribers, and came to wield as much influence in its area as the *Wall Street Journal*. In politics, it became clear that twentysomething Congressional aides were more likely to read Politico than traditional news magazines. In the media world, blogs and digital newsletters like paidcontent.org and Jim Romanesko replaced publications like *Editor and Publisher, Hollywood Reporter,* and *Ad Week,* all of which have fallen on hard times. In the sports world, fans turned in huge numbers to sites like deadspin.com and to the personal Twitter feeds of athletes, where even the mainstream press have started to get their "scoops."

New-media campaigns began to have more impact than traditional media ones. As Michael Terpin, a longtime new-media public relations entrepreneur who has started and grown two firms, told me, if you can get a story on the right blog, 500 other bloggers will link to it. "The overall effect on Google and traffic of a . . . a well-read thought leader can be more important than a large campaign to traditional media. We've had time after time where we could track far more response from a blog than from the *Today Show* or *USA Today* on the same story."

Not only did the rise of bloggers increase the number of places to get a message out or launch a product, it also began to shift the source of trust and authority from institutions (the big newspapers, news programs, or publishers, for example) to individuals. Financial journalist Matt Marshall, who had written about venture capital for the *San Jose Mercury News,* quit his newspaper job to found the VentureBeat blog and website. His audience for the blog grew bigger than any he had reached through the paper. In 2008, when the *New York Times* called VentureBeat one of the "best blogs on the Web," it began to run VentureBeat's articles on its own site. Marshall exemplifies how the source of clout has shifted. He built the audience on his own and then the newspaper came calling, asking to share it.

For people working in media at the time, as I was, the rise of this alternative group of solo curators was revolutionary. There was a lot of heady talk about "the democratization of news," but the biggest change was still to come. While anyone *could* start a blog, most people didn't—and even if someone did, who read it? Like the VCR, the blog in the early years was a technological underachiever, with less impact than it might have had, because it was inconvenient to use. At first, it required a basic comfort with simple computer programming, including the HTML formatting language that most people never developed. And so the democratization was stunted.

That changed with the rise of free, user-friendly blog-hosting platforms such as WordPress and blogspot, create-your-own-blog tools and hosting on Yahoo and Google, and social networks. Because they allowed amateurs to link to content in all its forms— video, audio, still photos, articles, websites, other blogs, and microblogs—these convergent sites turned their users into their own small-scale media gatekeepers, what we could call microcurators. If a thousand vampire enthusiasts scattered around the world link to the web page of an unknown self-published vampire novel, and each of them has a hundred friends or followers who click on that link, they can get that self-published novel more attention than most books from major publishers ever receive. And while most microcurators have a far smaller audience than larger curators in the media ecosystem, there are far more of them. When they find content compelling enough, they can link to it, repost it, retweet it, or rework it into their own new co-created forms, until the combined impact of their endorsements becomes more influential than the authority of any single individual or institution. Now the established curators—both traditional journalists and established, large-scale bloggers—must win the trust support of the microcurators. The advice that Mediaite.com editor Rachel Sklar offered journalists applies to anyone with a message to spread: "Wrote a story for the paper? Good, now put it on Facebook and tweet it out and make a companion YouTube video—and don't forget to Digg it!"

Information not only travels faster, it moves in a compressed, multimedia form. Where press releases were once modeled on newspaper articles, with a headline and an "inverted pyramid" of several paragraphs to explain the story, it's now necessary to compress that story into a tiny smartphone screen, as the little screen may be all that bloggers or journalists ever see. Sheila Morris, CEO of Morris Marketing and Entertainment, which markets U.S. television programming internationally, says, "I will spend a half hour figuring out how my subject line should read. I have to get the whole story into a headline and two sub-headings or a tweet." All of journalism's old who-what-when-where now has to fit on that small screen.

But while the changes in media have required adjustments for practitioners of PR, they haven't changed the basic PR transaction. As Richard Edelman told me, "Advertising is a one-way: Talk at. PR is a two way: Talk with. And it's always been true." To succeed at PR, you always had to be one voice among many, serving as a curator who offered up content. Now that word of mouth is the most powerful force in marketing, the essential question is how to reverse-engineer your conversations with curators both large and small. How do you get people who can talk about anything to talk about you? The answer is to offer them something new and interesting to say—to chat about, blog about, tweet about, and spread the word about in all media, new and old and in between.

That doesn't necessarily require a PR firm, but it helps to use a PR approach.

INFLUENCE, NOT CONTROL

The actress Megan Fox recently had a public and ugly feud with Michael Bay, her director in the *Transformers* movies. Fox is one of the most successful one-person brands on the planet, the subject of constant professional and amateur media attention. If anyone is positioned to win a global publicity fight, it would seem to be her. Yet even with her sway over media forms both new and old, she couldn't take control of her story. "Sometimes," she told the *New York Times Magazine,* "I so desperately want to clarify. I recently had an urge to get a Twitter account to explain myself. But me contradicting a news story is not going to make my words fact. It will just create a new news story. There's no solving this; it's completely its own monster. You have to come up with clever ways of getting your control back." In the past, a journalistic story was the final word. The paper was printed and couldn't be changed. Similarly, a personal or corporate embarrassment could—sometimes—be controlled with a firm, repeated, "No comment." Now, when a story breaks, the journalist or blogger's version is only the beginning—the power is now shared between the speaker and the audience, and the audience will respond and elaborate on the story the journalist has begun—or start new stories themselves. PR is at best a shared conversation, and while individuals and companies can influence that conversation, they can't control it.

The secret to wielding that influence is to cultivate an ongoing relationship with an audience that predisposes them to listen. Just as with advertising, combating a PR disaster means giving an audience reasons to *want* to listen. One of the "clever ways" is to show respect for the audience by responding quickly. When a blogger posted a video showing how to pick a Kryptonite bike lock with a ballpoint pen, decades of carefully built trust among urban cyclists began to turn to Internet outrage. The company was slow to respond, and as the damaging facts seemed to be followed by arrogant silence, the resulting publicity nearly destroyed them.

By contrast, when Pepsico offered an iPhone app that was widely criticized as offensive to women, they reacted quickly and with high sensitivity to the audience they were trying to reach. The app was a promotion for the Amp energy drink, and it was called "Amp Up Before You Score." It divided women into twenty-four categories, from Aspiring Actress to Treehugger, offered suggested pick-up lines for approaching each "type," and provided tools for users to post details of their "conquests" to a Brag List they could share through social networks.

Pepsi responded to the media outcry with an apology on Twitter: "Our app tried 2 show the humorous lengths guys go 2 pick up women. We apologize if it's in bad taste & appreciate your feedback." It linked the apology to a Twitter hashtag called "pepsifail," inviting further discussion on Twitter. Many bloggers and news stories praised Pepsi for their sensitive response, noting that by creating the hashtag they had shown an understanding of how their target audience likes to communicate, even if it perpetuated awareness of their gaffe.

Acknowledging a mistake can be as powerful in a relationship with consumers as it is in personal relationships. Almost everyone I know who travels frequently seems to have a story about choosing a hotel or restaurant *because* it made a mistake—and then quickly acknowledged it and worked to set it right. "We checked out your complaint, you're right; sorry, we'll take care of it" are powerful and calming words. That a company responds in itself is persuasive.

Yet some saw a subtler and less admirable PR effort at work in Pepsi's handling of the Amp app. David Coursey speculated on PCWorld.com that the entire incident, from the creation of the app through the apology, might have been a planned publicity scheme. He noted that even though Pepsi issued its apology, the company was slow to remove the offending app from the iPhone store, and speculated that Pepsi was still encouraging its young male customers to use and spread the app even as it apologized to those who found it offensive. I have no inside knowledge of the Pepsi campaign, but I can imagine how such a double-edged campaign might work for another company: Insult one group in a way that appeals to another group, then appeal to that second group by offering an apology for the insult. Then use the entire controversy to build the image of the overall brand as hip and sensitive. It would be naïve to think that every "conversation" with consumers in the C-scape will be straightforward and honest.

CAMPAIGNS ARE FOR THE LONG TERM

It seemed as if the first thing older people worried about in regard to MySpace, Facebook, and similar sites was that they could be a threat to younger people's careers if their youthful excesses were preserved online and visible to future employers. Yet while many teenagers were warned of these dangers, adults and their companies didn't always seem to realize that the Internet also preserved their past attempts at marketing. Old campaigns live on even as companies try to launch new ones. Sheila Morris told me this story, disguising the names of the companies at the request of her client:

I was approached by Company B, a new company, looking for a public relations campaign to launch and announce their new endeavor. Company B is an international television distribution company specializing in documentary programming with a slate of titles in its library. We prepared a press release outlining the new, existing, and in-production programs, along with an executive summary of the leading execs. In order to garner a significant story, we decided to offer an "exclusive" interview to one of the leading journalists covering documentary programming. We sent all of the completed documents to this journalist. . . . But our initial follow-up calls were not returned, alerting me to the fact that something was amiss. Journalists live for exclusive stories! Once I finally connected with the journalist, I was made aware of the fact that the leading executive from Company B had previously been with Company A and that all of the titles had previously been announced under Company A. According to the journalist, there was nothing "new" here and he was not interested in the story.

In the C-scape, a quick Internet search would have revealed the history of those titles and the lack of candor from the new client.

The speed of new-media technologies gives a false impression that anything can be handled in a few minutes from a laptop or a BlackBerry, but it has become crucial that your marketing campaigns are consistent with the long-term goals of the brand. "We're not even publicists anymore," Morris told me. "I'm a strategist. I get a lot of last-minute phone calls [from people launching companies] but I can't take a last-minute client. I'm going to do them a disservice. I have to know your company as well as you do."

VIRAL MARKETING—PR BY NEW MEANS

To see just how resilient the methods of PR will remain despite—and in fact, because of—the era of the C-scape, let's compare two examples, one decades old and one recent. Back in 1986, when I was executive editor of the *San Francisco Examiner*, we had ambitions to fight back against television news and increase our readership. We wanted to create television ads and get ourselves exposure, but we couldn't afford a lot of TV. We went to a brand new agency in California, Goodby, Berlin and Silverstein, and we said, "Look, we only have a paltry amount of money in our ad budget. How can we compete?" They said we could afford to buy three local ads in prime time, but no more than that. We asked them, what do we do to leverage those buys to get us more exposure?

Their idea was to insult TV news on TV. Buy ads in the middle of news broadcasts and during an NFL game and insult the TV news broadcasts. I said, come on! They said, trust us. So they made some inexpensive and insulting ads. In one, a Barbie doll and a Ken doll sit at an anchor desk on the set of TV news show. The tag line was something like: "The San Francisco Examiner: we have news, they don't." For the second ad, a camera crew went to the top of Coit Tower in San Francisco and dropped a television and a newspaper. But the film was doctored so the newspaper dropped like a rock and cracked the sidewalk. The TV just floated down like a feather. The point was to show that TV news had no substance. The last ad was a billboard with photos of Ken and Barbie behind a news desk with a tag line that read, "TV news is an oxymoron."

We ran these ads just a few times, quickly spending through

our budget. If our competitors at the local television stations had only ignored us, we wouldn't have been able to say any more. So although technically this was advertising—we paid for three appearances in prime time—that extremely brief ad "campaign" was just a way to get the media gatekeepers' attention.

They might have just ignored us, but they didn't. Instead, they took the bait. Every local television station in the San Francisco area did a story about the ads, to "rebut" them. One even took a helicopter and dropped their own TV and newspaper from the air, filming their fall to demonstrate for their viewers that in fact a television falls faster and hits the ground harder than a newspaper—in case anyone didn't know that already. Then the major television networks picked up the stories from the local stations and ran them nationally—including our ads, which were seen across the country. We got millions of dollars worth of free air time because our agency understood the communications ecosystem. They knew who the relevant curators were in the 1980s—television news executives—and what would provoke them to spend time spreading "our" word about our newspaper.

Now jump forward three decades to 2009, when digital videos began appearing on YouTube, showing a man running through well-known locations in New York City, wearing nothing but running shoes, socks, and a fanny pack that he had moved, thoughtfully, to the front. Styling himself "the world's fastest nudist," he built himself an audience through word of mouth and mentions on popular blogs including Gothamist, Gawker, and Huffington Post. The *Park Slope Courier* published an interview with the runner, who said that he had won the World Nude 10K race in Barcelona, Spain. *Anderson Cooper 360* on CNN broadcast one of his videos, with Mr. Cooper joking, "This does not faze New Yorkers—believe me we have all seen much worse than this."

However, the series of videos was not one runner's documents of his odd obsession. It was a scripted campaign for Zappos, the online supplier of clothing and footwear, designed to promote their "blazing fast delivery of clothes and shoes." In later videos a truck full of Zappos employees drove up to dress the naked runner with clothes from Zappos. The rest was fiction: there is no World Nude 10K race in Barcelona or anywhere else (as the writer at the *Park Slope Courier* could have found out with a simple Internet search), and the nude champion runner was in fact a New York actor wearing sheer panty hose and an item called a "Houdini" to comply— barely—with the city's nudity laws. The viral campaign, created by the company Agent 16, became legendary.

Of course, there are differences between the *San Francisco Examiner*'s floating television spot and the Zappos online videos, both in terms of the technologies used (television versus viral video) and the curators targeted (television news editors versus bloggers, informal net surfers, and, as a side bonus, TV and print news reporters). At the *Examiner*, we made a small purchase of advertising time—in a strictly economic sense, we weren't doing PR, or at least not until our ad budget ran out—while Zappos relied entirely on public postings. But the underlying methods for reaching and engaging an audience were the same. In both cases, the agencies behind the campaigns understood the communications ecosystem well enough to win the attention they wanted from the curators by offering compellingly outrageous content that worked on two levels. When you first saw the newspaper crack the sidewalk or the naked jogger run by, it was absurd—it made almost anyone want to say, "Did you see that? That can't be right! Look again!" Then, when the audience understood that it was faked and why, it became an in-joke that united the viewer and the sponsor. That in-joke became the basis of an enjoyable relationship between the sponsor and the viewer, which readied the viewer for the product pitch that followed.

Underneath the new technology, a viral marketing campaign such as Zappos' naked jogger or Burger King's "Subservient Chicken" website, is a PR campaign, one aimed not at media institutions but at microcurators. And despite the changes in technologies and the new curators, the underlying skills haven't changed much, whether you're sponsoring the local opera house or posting fake videos of a streaker. (This may explain why the skills that Sheila Morris looks for when she's hiring for her PR agency haven't changed much, either. Topping her list are "business sense," "common sense," "good writing ability," and "social skills." The rest, she says—including web skills—she can teach.)

Here are three examples of successful convergent PR in a single industry, banking. Nicolet National Bank was a small community bank in Wisconsin without the resources to compete with its much larger and better-known competitors. One day, Jeff J. Gahnz, vice president of marketing and public relations, sat in on a meeting with his CEO, who was explaining a complex point about banking in a strikingly clear and enjoyable way. Gahnz appreciated the CEO's effective, accessible explanation, and realized his customers would, too. Here was something Nicolet could offer that bigger banks couldn't: hear the CEO speak on practical topics that concerned customers. The bank began offering his ideas to customers on blogs, audio and video podcasts, and on a community hub called "The Vault." Customers could share this information with friends and family, and in this way the bank became a source of high-quality financial content for its customers, and the customers became a network of microbloggers who shared the bank's unique, useful, and user-friendly content.

First National Bank of Omaha, an online bank, took a convergent PR approach to spreading the word about how to maximize interest on the money in customer accounts. A useful but not scintillating topic, it was unlikely to generate a lot of buzz on its own. So the bank created a kind of online reality program that they called the "Pay Yourself First Challenge." Would-be contestants were invited to post a video on YouTube in which they described their financial situations and their saving goals. Five contestants were selected to blog about their progress, and the bank chose a winner based on both their success in reaching their goals and voting by the online audience. In this way, some rather dry content about how online accounts could improve interest rates became part of a more compelling drama co-created by an audience of existing and potential FNBO customers.

Citi Credit Cards, meanwhile, knew that many of their existing customers had Facebook accounts, and that a referral from an existing customer was a powerful way to win a new customer. But what would give customers a reason to promote Citi Credit Cards when they were free to post on Facebook about whatever they liked? Rather than trying to wear their customers down with repeated ads (difficult to do on Facebook, where the ads are small and shunted to the side of the screen), they offered to donate $50 to a charity of the customer's choice for each approved credit card application he or she referred. The campaign, called, "Make a Difference, One Friend at a Time," gave customers a reason to promote Citi's charitable giving. It was a PR campaign that turned the bank's existing customers into a crowdsourced marketing department, identifying new customers, crafting personalized messages to them, and directing them to the Citi Credit website.

These examples show three different, lower-cost ways that banks have offered to compensate potential customers for their attention: with entertainment, with useful information, and with cash (for a cause). All three approaches increased awareness of the banks' services, and went even further, engaging their audience with personal benefits. All three of these approaches avoided the pitfalls of traditional advertising and saved marketing dollars at the same time. Even the $50 that Citibank paid to charities selected by Facebook users was equal to or lower than the cost to the bank of getting a new cardholder from any other source, such as paid advertising, direct mail, or even Internet advertising.

THE 80–20 RULE GOES VIRAL

What if you can't afford to target all your existing or potential customers equally? Advertising guru Jon Bond recommends a strategy based on an updated version of the "80–20 rule" that marketing professors have taught for years. The old principle held that, typically, 80 percent of your sales come from only 20 percent of your customers. The most famous campaign designed to take advantage of this insight was the old Rheingold commercial that declared it "the one beer to have when you're having more than one." The goal was to appeal to the heavy beer drinker (20 percent of beer drinkers) by claiming that the flavor held up beer after beer—something that biologists claim is impossible. Nevertheless, many in that 20 percent subset of beer drinkers began drinking it by the case, making Rheingold a success, without relying on the other 80 percent of the market.

Surprisingly, according to Bond, the 80–20 principle also applies to that most-valuable 20 percent, meaning that 20 percent of the 20 percent (4 percent) accounts for 64 percent of your business. And the new twist is that the people who typically participate in viral marketing are also the heavy users of a brand, who are the most committed, knowledgeable, and vocal about "their" brand.

"Instead of talking to everyone," Bond told me, "wouldn't you want to spend your time learning everything about these super customers and then modeling them against the rest of the population to find a few more of these golden geese? So, the game is becoming identifying them and then finding out so much about them that you can literally build a one to one relationship with them, akin to have a salesperson knock on their door."

Jean-Christophe Bedos, president of Boucheron, took this approach when his company opened its first store in Shanghai. At the time, there was a boom in luxury brands in China, and many brands were building big, impressive stores in major Chinese cities. As part of planning for the opening of the new Boucheron store, Bedos made a trip to meet Chinese consumers and clients of major luxury brands. One of them complained to him about luxury brands from the West. The man said that he was on the lists PR companies made, so he got invited to every store launch party. The format, he complained, was always the same. He was invited to two or three opening parties a week, sometimes two in a day, and at each one he was expected to come to the store, eat some peanuts or some canapés, drink a glass of champagne, hear a little speech or watch a little demonstration, and go home.

He said that, in China, if you are a tycoon and you want to show people you have wealth, you invite them to a big lunch or a big dinner. You do something that will impress them. Bedos came home and told his marketing people that instead of the usual event for the Boucheron store opening, he wanted to organize a dinner with champagne, caviar, foie gras, and so on. Instead of inviting two hundred, they would invite twenty hand-picked potential ambassadors for the company and give them an experience worth talking about. Since then, says Bedos, when the company opens a store or launches a new line, they spend less money and time

courting the press and more making their most desirable customers ambassadors.

Canadian Club whisky's campaign with the charity Movember shows how a variety of different PR approaches, both old and
new, can be combined to intensify word of mouth for a brand and
inspire new ambassadors. Movember is a charity that works to
inform men about prostate and testicular cancer and raise funds
for research. To make that serious subject more fun, they challenge men to grow moustaches during the month of November
and to ask others to sponsor their efforts by making donations
to the charity. Canadian Club recognized that the profile of the
men who joined Movember matched their target audience for the
whisky. The company became a major sponsor of the charity and
partnered with Movember in a social media campaign.

One app on the whisky company's Facebook page, "Which Mo
Are You?" suggested moustache styles for men to try, based on
a personality test. Another, "Mo Your Friends," enabled users to
draw moustaches on photos from their Facebook albums, showing how they and their friends might look if they joined the cause,
and giving Facebook users an excuse to draw on each other's photographs. Participants who raised at least a hundred dollars for the
charity during the month of "Movember" were invited to attend
one of several celebratory parties across the United States, where
they were served "Burgundys," a new Canadian Club cocktail.
Participants' moustaches were judged and awarded prizes, and
these "superfans" then pasted photos and accounts of the event to
the Facebook page. Over the course of the campaign, Canadian
Club's new Facebook page grew to nearly 16,000 fans.

7

DIGITAL MINDREADING

CUSTOMER SERVICE REPLACES SALES

Talk to anyone who had a flight cancelled and was entitled to a refund from an airline over the past twenty years. Even if the airline acknowledged that they owed you money, they would have offered you a trip voucher or coupon that could only be used if you met certain criteria and were willing to come to an airline office. At the office, often no one could figure out when the voucher could be applied or deal with the inconvenience associated with cashing in the refund. Similarly, every traveler had an airline lost-baggage horror story, a mix of bad luck and bad personal treatment. And if you received horrible, beyond-the-pale customer service, what could you do? Make phone calls, write a letter, complain to friends—in other words, not much. With effort you might get some personal satisfaction, but you couldn't have much effect on the company overall.

That was the old approach to customer service, and it did not change magically with the rise of the Internet. Even early versions of successful online companies ignored their customers. One of the worst customer service functions existed at America Online.

It was well known that a subscriber trying to cancel AOL Internet service would find that simple transaction impossible to complete. You had to call over and over again to reach a representative. When you got through, it became obvious that representatives were compensated based on preventing customers from cancelling their subscriptions. AOL made a small fortune on people paying well beyond the time they stopped using the service.

In that environment, when a company did emphasize customer service, it became news. Companies like Dell and Southwest Airlines built reputations by not treating their customers badly, and this approach was frequently fodder for a magazine profile of an "unusual strategy." Yet in recent years, consumers' increased power, and the broader marketing changes within the C-scape, have changed customer service from an afterthought to a necessity.

There are three reasons companies feel increasing pressure to provide better customer service:

- **Increased competition among brands of all kinds.** Digital technologies have lowered the costs of entering almost every type of business, and the Internet, of course, has made it easier for anyone to compare different offerings. With more choice and greater ease in shopping of all kinds, consumers can select the company that offers better customer service. Younger airlines such as JetBlue have won market share by offering consumer-friendly services, like handling refunds and bonus points electronically on the web, convenient for their customers to use when they book their next flight. In the same way, technology has ended the monopoly the cable company has over its viewers. We don't need the cable company to get the full range of choices on television, we can choose a satellite provider, a phone company, or an online provider; instead of jokes about our dependence on the "cable guy," you're much more likely to hear people sharing stories about cancelling cable service altogether.

- **Companies rely on their customers almost as employees.** In the era of the C-scape, companies rely on customers not just to buy products or services but to give word of mouth recommendations, review performance, provide quality control by testing beta products, contribute to product design, and be co-creators, co-marketers, and quasi-employees. As Jean-Christophe Bedos, president of Boucheron, points out, there was once a hierarchy of customers, the "nobility" who paid retail and the illegitimate children, the "bastards," who bought your product through a third-party discounter. "Now it's about your bastards," Bedos said. "You in your castle have official and unofficial children. So do you accept that they are your children? Do you give them customer service if something is broken? Do you honor the warranty?"

  While some people in his industry would say that those who don't pay full price shouldn't be treated as full clients, Bedos disagrees. "If they wear your product, they are your ambassadors, because no one will ever ask someone if they paid full price for their watch." Creating word of mouth means taking care of everyone who might have a story to tell about it.

- **"Wherever, however shopping" means you must service even *potential* customers.** Even customers who already know they want to buy from you have far more ways to reach you and to do business with you than ever before. They may shop in person or by mail or by phone, on your website or by comparing prices with search engines or by referrals from blogs and social media pages. They may prefer to shop with their smartphones' shopping apps. They expect to shop at any time, from wherever they happen to be, on whatever device seems most convenient, and they reserve the right not to commit—their preferences may change again three months from now. And the impact of these shifts can be seismic: when Harvard Business School Press e-books became available not just on e-readers like the Kindle but on the iPhone's Kindle app, that one improvement in the convenience they could offer potential customers caused e-book sales to triple.

People increasingly multitask as they shop—shopping while at work or while they take care of their children or commute—while some people still enjoy the personal relationship they can only have by shopping with a knowledgeable salesperson who may have connections to a products' designers and craftspeople. An increasing number of people defy categorization, so they have to be reached on multiple levels. "Wherever, however shopping," as Bedos calls it, means that an enormous new burden of responsibility has shifted to retailers. Companies must track all the still-evolving ways a potential customer might do business with them, and work to improve the experience of consumers who have browsed but not yet made a purchase. While traditional customer service used to be an obligation to a limited number of customers in a narrow window of time—between the sale and the expiration of the return period or the warranty period—what we could call "potential-customer service" is an ongoing requirement for every consumer who might even consider you.

Living up to this requirement can be a challenge for companies who have not made customer service a priority. Early in 2009, for example, the executives at Weather.com, the website run by the Weather Channel, found that growth in visits to their site, the industry leader for weather news and information, flattened out. At first they assumed they were losing to their competition, but when they looked to their major competitors, they found something strange: the competitors were also flat. Just about everyone in the weather category had also stopped growing on the web. What was happening?

Consumers were shifting their information gathering from computers to mobile phones. The iPhone had made its debut and phone apps were growing wildly. In just one year, use of the web from mobile phones had jumped 30 percent. Weather.com had created a great iPhone application for weather that was easier to use than the website—so much easier that hundreds of thousands of mobile users were switching to the Weather.com app, making it one of the most popular on the iPhone.

But while the tech people at the company had designed a great app, no one had figured out how to monetize it. The website sold ads at a good clip, but apps were new territory. So the marketers at Weather.com were still spending all their time trying to get everyone to use their website. My message to them: you're ignoring a clear message from your customers. They want to get their weather information on their mobile devices. Don't direct people away from your biggest area of growth. Pounce on that mobile growth, expand your mobile offerings, and find ways to monetize this new platform. If you can't service these customers the way they want to be serviced, they'll go elsewhere.

In the same way, Boucheron needed to better service customers who didn't necessarily want to buy their perfume and jewelry in the traditional way, by traveling to a high-end store. These potential customers still wanted to see Boucheron's offerings, but some felt better served if they had the option to examine them on a computer screen in 3D video so they could shop from their home or hotel room. Some might still want to talk to an informed salesperson who was familiar with the materials and the designers that made the products unique, but they felt better served if they could reach that salesperson on a telephone hotline. Boucheron's CEO told me he didn't know which of these methods would create the most sales, but he knew that the choice does not belong to the brand anymore. It belongs to the consumer.

NOT A DEPARTMENT, A MIND-SET

For all three of these reasons, the afterthought that used to be the customer service department has become one of the most important functions of any company, another "line of business," a constant activity that begins before any given customer makes a purchase and never ends. Success means not just making sales but providing satisfying overall customer experiences, through ongoing contact with your customers and sensitivity to their changing needs.

This approach may require changing company attitudes about customers at every level, from salespeople to top management, and fostering a new attention and respect for the customer experience. I remember that attitude was missing years ago when I took over as editor of the *San Francisco Examiner*. Early on, I met with the top people in the circulation department. Since the *Examiner* was an afternoon newspaper (remember those, anyone?) that sold about half of its copies each day at newsstands or out of newspaper racks (as opposed to copies delivered to homes), it was important for the salespeople in circulation to work with editorial to present the most appealing front page.

The circulation managers came to me with a strategy for increasing afternoon sales. They pointed out that when the paper ran larger headlines, it sold more copies. Their request was simple: Make the letters bigger. Run larger headlines.

I could understand their logic from the point of view of making a sale. A customer who saw a big banner headline would be likely to pick it up, today. But circulation had never asked the consumer why he was buying that newspaper with the big headlines. It wasn't because the letters were large. It was because the story was an interesting, important one that deserved a large headline. Circulation was ignoring the fundamental relationship between the paper and its readers. Our readership trusted us to highlight major stories, to put things into a context by telling them: something major has happened, and you need to read about it. We only screamed with large type when the news warranted it. If we screamed all the time like the boy who cried "wolf," our audience would stop believing us. It would only take a few days of inflated headlines on not-so-large stories before readers stopped believing any large headlines we wrote.

To make my point, I had the composing room set a front page with a huge headline that said: WEATHER'S FINE. When the circulation department saw it, they laughed—it wasn't that they were incapable of understanding that no one would be excited to buy a huge headline on a small story; they just hadn't seen that kind of thinking about the customer experience as part of their job. Yet our long-term sales depended on providing an ongoing experience of well-curated news that our customers could rely on.

PERFECT SERVICE IS SERVICE BEFORE THEY ASK FOR IT

Digital technologies have made it possible to service a customer's ongoing needs in ways that were barely imaginable a few years ago. Hulu, the website that distributes television programming and other video from Fox, NBC, and ABC, has sped up and simplified the process of fixing a problem with their service by using social networks to save customers the trouble of contacting customer service at all. As CEO Jason Kilar told Charlie Rose, he spends a huge amount of time monitoring Twitter feeds and other online outlets that reveal customers' experience of Hulu in real time. If a feature on the site, big or small, isn't working, someone will complain about it on a social network. So Hulu makes it their business to listen in.

"What I do," Kilar told Rose, "is I go to search.twitter.com, and I search for the name 'Hulu.' I do that about twenty times a day, because the name 'Hulu' gets written about on Twitter about 2,400 times a day right now."

Rose asked, "You can't read 2,400 [posts] a day, can you?"

"It turns out you can," Kilar responded. "As long as you look at it every twenty minutes. So I have a Blackberry and I look at it every twenty minutes. And I'm not the only one. Almost everybody at Hulu looks. . . . And the reason we do it is that it is real-time feedback on the quality of the customer experience that we're delivering. So, we're able to know if we're doing something right and double down on it. We're able to know if we misspelled a word on a Web site . . . and we'll know instantly."

Of course, instant knowledge is only an advantage if you can react to it quickly. "There are many occasions where at 11:45 at night, I'll see a tweet about, say, a word that was misspelled, for example, on the website. I'll be able to send that to our CTO Eric, and he and I will have a conversation at 11:47 at night, and the site will be fixed by midnight. That's a 15-minute turnaround, where without Twitter, that wasn't possible. It's an amazing transparency engine."

Responding to a flaw in a customer's experience within fifteen minutes is a dramatic improvement in speed, but even more important is the shift in responsibility for the customer's experience. No Hulu customer had to locate a customer service email address or make his way, annoyed, through the steps of an automated phone menu to complain about a problem on the site. The company was eavesdropping on whatever its customers cared to say, and made it their business to respond to what they overheard. The person who complained might not even know that he or she was the reason the problem got corrected.

Bad customer service experiences always have one element in common: they waste your time. But social networking has the promise to transform customer service into a kind of collective digital mindreading, in which your company overhears what makes customers unhappy when they're still just griping about it to their Twitter followers, before they're even bothered enough to make a formal customer service request—and then, they discover, the problem is almost magically solved without requiring any time at all.

THE FUTURE: "CONCIERGE" SALES

Customer service exists because there are customers having a bad experience with a purchase: the customer may feel dissatisfied and frustrated, and she wants that feeling to end. In a similar way, customers who want a product or service that they don't yet have are also having a bad experience. They feel the lack of the product they want, they know it's going to take time and understanding to correct it, but they would prefer to be satisfied right now. In that sense, every shopper needs customer service, if only someone would provide it. Of course, they can browse, they can search online, they can ask real and virtual friends, but what they desire—even if it hasn't occurred to them to ask—is for a curator to appear as if by magic, a trusted resource, a kind of personal shopper or lifestyle concierge who knows their preferences and offers suggestions as reliably as a close friend.

This approach explains an important part of the success of Amazon.com as compared to brick-and-mortar department stores. A traditional store, no matter how well it understands its customers, still has to pick one layout on any given day, featuring some products and not others. The online superstore not only offers a much larger variety of content, and a user-friendly interface for finding, comparing, and ordering that content; it also rearranges the store every time a new customer walks in. By keeping a record of what you have ordered previously, it can make recommendations based on your past behavior. What I see when I go to the site and look through the virtual "aisles" is different from what you see. And as Jeffrey Rayport, who worked with Amazon, points out, it's a zero-variable-cost proposition: the algorithms running in the Amazon data centers have already been written, and it doesn't cost the company to redesign the layout of their products. Amazon can create a unique store for each one of its 70 million customers.

But if Amazon and other online superstores have taken steps in the direction of offering a "mindreading" experience of concierge marketing, no one has gotten all the way there. The difficulty is that there is so much the site doesn't know about its customers. If I order a gift for an associate's child, Amazon may continue to offer me suggestions based on that kid's taste for years—possibly longer than the relationship will last, and certainly longer than that type of book or game I bought as a gift will be right for that kid as he or she continues to grow. Even if the site could keep straight what I bought to keep for myself and what to give to others, for every item I buy from Amazon, there are many more I already own or purchased elsewhere, and the only way to let the website know is to painstakingly enter and rate every other item in that category, something no one takes the time to do. And even if the site knew everything I owned, it would continue to make suggestions of movies with actors I'd tired of, hobbies I'd given up, and so on.

A similar problem exists with Google AdSense. If I'm emailing with my friend about how much we love or hate New York Yankee hitters, an ad may pop up offering to sell me a Yankee jersey. That may feel in the moment like a brilliant bit of mindreading, one that leads me to buy a shirt I didn't even realize I wanted until the site suggested it to me. On the other hand, if I'm doing a search to find out who wrote the old Andrews Sisters hit about "working for the Yankee dollar," I may also be sent the same ad offering me the same Yankee baseball jersey, and my only response to AdSense then will be to shake my head and laugh. Overall, observing customer behavior is important to your ongoing relationship, but it's not enough to allow you to offer true "concierge" sales.

Does anyone get this balance right? In traditional retail, the most successful area—and the exception to the rule that traditional businesses didn't care about customer service—was small, high-end businesses that depended on a limited clientele. Gourmet restaurants, for example, where the headwaiter and the sommelier remembered every dish you ever ordered and every wine you ever drank, and telephoned or sent a card to let you know what they'd bought for their cellar recently or that the truffles were in from Italy. Similarly, there were small, elite clothing or import boutiques that made it their business to know the tastes of a relatively small number of customers, and to contact them regularly with suggestions for the new season. That wine steward or boutique owner was doing two things: observing what you bought from him or her, but also getting to know you and your interests more broadly. That made it possible to curate for each potential customer *individually,* viewing each as a unique market segment of one, and then making recommendations accordingly. There was no need to show you a menu or ask you questions.

ANSWER BEFORE THEY ASK

It's possible to do even better than remembering customers' past preferences. Because social network users make enormous amounts of personal information about their interests public (their jobs, leisure activities, professional affiliations, memberships, likes and dislikes, favorite places to travel, and so on, endlessly), social networks offer a rich information mine for advertisers who want to match ads with the people who would be most interested in them. The brands don't have to wait until the potential customers enter terms in search engines—their interests are already posted online. According to Tim Kendall, Facebook's director of monetization, "The marketing slogan that we use is 'Find your customers before they search.'"

When the Veneto Casino in Panama grew disappointed with the response it was getting to traditional advertisements (on bus shelters, in airports, in travel guides, and with travel agents) to attract visitors to its 150-room hotel, CEO Andrew Silverman went looking for a way to put his ads in front of true potential customers—and not just anyone looking to take a bus or a plane somewhere. Silverman hired a small but feisty start-up digital marketing firm in New York City, Crossborders, to help figure out how to target the right customers. The Crossborders team set him up with the Facebook Ad Network that allowed him to target specific neighborhoods in several countries in South America where people's interests matched the profiles of Veneto guests. They showed him how he could monitor the performance of his ads in real time and make changes in his ad spending based on how the ads were performing. If one ad in one area was leading to bookings, it would allow him to spend more on showing that ad to users with similar interests, so that the suggestion of a casino vacation in Panama appeared before the eyes of exactly those users who might find it most charming.

Silverman stayed on Facebook all weekend, adjusting the audience type he wanted to attract to the hotel in real time, watching the ad pricing, and jumping on opportunities. He cleaned up. For only $2,000, he filled his hotel's rooms in two hours, and stopped advertising. "He is on Facebook all day long watching the pricing of his ads, playing with the demographics and constantly just tweaking and taking advantage of the Facebook ad system," said Nick Godfey, co-CEO of Crossborders. "He is a prime example of a CEO who has embraced New Media." Silverman believes he has found his natural calling—selling by recognizing his customers' needs even before they do.

When this approach succeeds, it not only means an end to forcing the customer into the purchase funnel, trying to push him into awareness and consideration on the marketer's terms; it also means offering to take on the longer-term work of consideration, answering questions for the consumer that the consumer used to ask him- or herself: What would I like next? What's missing from my life? What would make me happy?

At its best, for the consumer, concierge marketing produces none of the unpleasant friction of the hard sell. As advertising guru Jon Bond puts it, "Everyone hates selling and no one wants to be 'sold.' Selling and all the clichés of Willy Loman that accompany it will start to disappear, replaced by service."

PART THREE

WHAT HAPPENS TO PRODUCTS?

8

IS EVERYTHING "CONTENT"?

EVERY PRODUCT IS NOW A MEDIA EXPERIENCE

"Everyone knew" it couldn't be done. You couldn't sell shoes on the Internet. Shoes were not like books or toothbrushes—a description and a picture posted online wouldn't make consumers feel confident enough to buy. A numeric shoe size didn't tell you what you needed to know, because shoe sizes varied and feet varied even more. Shoppers needed to try shoes on, walk in them, check them out in the mirror. They needed to feel the leather or the suede. Pictures and even video couldn't tell them how they'd look walking or dancing or sitting in a pair of shoes. Footwear had to be sold in stores. "Everyone knew."

This fixed idea about a particular product was just one example of a much bigger idea that "everyone" also "knew": that there were three kinds of products.

- Digital products (online publications, music, video, bank accounts)
- Traditional products that could be sold online (packaged goods, groceries)

- Traditional products that could not be sold online (shoes, cars, doctor visits)

A fixed idea like that always seems to make sense until someone flattens it—and builds a billion-dollar business where it used to be. That's what Zappos did by selling shoes online. And when they did, they found an opportunity where others had seen only barriers and confusion—not just in terms of customer service (as the company famously describes its approach), but in the creation and re-creation of products themselves.

Everyone knew that consumers had always chosen to buy shoes in stores, but Zappos asked a deeper question about consumer choice: what were consumers choosing when they picked a specific shoe store? Newspaper companies always assumed that the news and the paper had to go together, until it turned out that many people were happy to get the news without the paper. In the same way, Zappos explored whether customers who had always chosen to shop at shoe stores wanted the store, or would they be just as happy—or happier—to skip the store and simply get the shoes.

Zappos' initial experiment—the heart of their business—was to offer "free" overnight shipping in both directions. This arrangement raised the company's costs, of course, compared to their competitors, but they were saving money associated with all the stores they didn't have to open—real estate costs, construction costs, labor costs, and marketing costs to drive customers to stores. Now it was possible to order shoes, try them on at home, and send them back if you didn't like them. Not only did the new approach let consumers bring home much of what they liked about shopping in a store, it also offered appealing benefits. A customer could try the shoes on with several different outfits, or wear them for a few hours to see if they stayed comfortable. By comparison, what a shoe store offered seemed rushed, crowded, and impersonal.

WHAT YOU SELL IS A CONSUMER EXPERIENCE

Zappos understood—or discovered along the way—that they were not in the shoe-store business. They were not even in the retail shoe business. They were in the convergent-shoe-shopping-experience business, and that included the shoes in the box; the overnight arrival; the reassuring promise of free return shipping (whether or not you used it); the easy-to-reach, helpful call center; the confidence-inspiring website with its mix of company-created and community-created content; and other elements that led a customer to open a box of footwear and feel good. The shoes, of course, were the essential core of that experience, but the shoes alone couldn't have done that. Every shoe retailer in the world had boxes of shoes.

IS IT ALL "CONTENT"?

That brings us back to the big wrong idea I mentioned at the start of this chapter. It seems sensible (and it feels reassuring) to go on seeing products as divided in three: digital content, traditional content that can be sold online, and traditional content that must be sold in traditional brick-and-mortar ways. But in the C-scape, how to understand what we sell is not our choice. It's the consumer's choice, and consumers don't separate out the parts of their experiences. What's in the box, what's on the website, what's said on the phone, how it feels to deal with the company, how confident a purchase makes buyers feel—all the different levels, traditional and digital, blur together. Not every product is digital, but that's not the point: it was always a misunderstanding to think that convergence meant that new technology would replace the old. New technology gets layered in with the old, and every experience of a product becomes a convergent experience, whether or not the product "is digital."

Do I really mean *every* product? If that's correct, it has huge implications for product development, customer retention, and even company organization. So let's take a look at some categories of product that would seem not to fit, to make sure the example of Zappos isn't some misleading exception.

Consider the plane ticket. Like a ticket for anything, it has always been a piece of media, traditionally printed on paper, increasingly replaced by "e-tickets." When a ticket-taker scans an e-ticket off a customer's phone and onto a digital ticket-taking device, boarding an airplane is about as pure a new-media experience as a person can have.

Of course, when someone says "plane ticket," they don't mean just the ticket. They mean the trip. Getting from here to there by sitting in a physical seat, on a non-digital, mostly metal airplane that flies through the vast, non-digital, non-convergent sky. Isn't that right?

Yes—but now we're no longer talking about a single, physical, non-media product. We're talking about an experience, one that unfolds over time as a result of many different elements. The airplane is a physical object, of a certain make and model, well maintained or not, flying directly or indirectly to where you need to go. You sit in a physical seat that has physical attributes: comfortable or not, quiet and conveniently placed for boarding and leaving the plane or in back near the restrooms amid the noise from the jet engine in the plane's tail. The seat you bought may entitle you to food and drink during the flight, or it may not. These are all non-media aspects of the flight, and they influence a customer's experience of flying and future decisions about which airline to fly and in which price class.

Yet even in what we could call the non-media "core" of the flying experience, there are media elements. Some flights offer duty-free catalog shopping from paper catalogs while you are in the air, a form of traditional commercial media. Some seats on airplanes provide no entertainment; some offer a single choice of movie; some offer a selection of movies, a DirectTV feed, and wireless Internet access. For me, on a long, cross-country flight, these media elements make a huge difference to my overall experience. In this sense, some people choose an airline offering in-flight television exactly as they choose an online newspaper over a traditional one: when the mood strikes, they can switch to video. I have even scheduled flights to coincide with a sporting event, so I could watch the whole game from my seat.

Beyond the literal media available on the flight, the experience of plane travel is shaped by all of the media involved in buying your ticket, selecting your seat, printing your boarding pass (or downloading it to your smartphone), moving through security, receiving information about delays or transfer gates, and so on. And before and after your actual flight, there is additional media messaging around the experience of being the airline's customer, including the ways the airline shapes its relationship with its customers by offering frequent-flyer points, access to a lounge, efforts to send you information and special offers relevant to your future travel, and so forth.

Travelers buy their tickets, board their planes, get to their destinations, and feel they had good flights or bad ones. Maybe they break out a few aspects of the experience that mattered most to them that day, but they don't perform a detailed analysis. I've done so here, though, to make two points:

- Even a "non-media" product such as transportation has multiple media layers, often more than consumers realize.
- A consumer's experience—and ultimate satisfaction—with your product will result from that blend of media and non-media elements, and he or she won't distinguish or care what is media related or not. It's the producer's job to get that blend right.

It's important to recognize that what you sell, whatever it is, must now have both media and non-media layers. I haven't stacked the deck with the examples I picked, both of which involve a lot of technology. Zappos relies on the Internet for sales and a sophisticated national transportation system for its overnight deliveries. Airplanes are, of course, a modern, high-tech invention. What about more traditional products?

Let's look at golf. A thoroughly non-digital game, based on hitting a ball into a hole with a stick, it has been played since at least the sixteenth century in Scotland—though it may have originated 500 years earlier during China's Song dynasty and migrated with Mongolian travelers to the Netherlands and then north. While the early origins of the game are disputed, everyone agrees it began a long time ago as an outdoor, non-media activity. In the C-scape, however, the golf experience is being reshaped by a variety of media, including a phone application called AccelGolf. Out on the golf course, the app turns your phone into a GPS rangefinder that measures yardage to the next hole and helps you set up your shot. It tracks your performance game by game and helps you plan workout routines to address your weak spots. It even breaks down your performance club by club, providing statistics on the impact of new purchases, and recommending equipment changes and alternative set-up in a feature called the "digital golf bag." It provides a database of information about golf courses all over the world, and access to an online community of golfers who can provide recommendations and advice about where to play and what you need to know when you get there—the company's marketing materials promise that the app "makes every course your home course."

Traditionalists might object that with all of this technical interference, this is no longer really golf, yet there were always experienced caddies who knew the course by heart and could calculate yardages by eye and give advice on setting up each shot. There were always pros who analyzed your game and suggested workouts; there were always social circles where other members would provide secrets to golf courses all around the world. Most people couldn't afford access to this game-enhancing information; the traditional form that this "golf media" took, in other words, was elite word of mouth. But it was always part of the game.

If you sell golf products in the era of AccelGolf and its various competitors, you will find that even that traditional game has become a hybrid of a sport and a digital media experience. If you manufacture clubs, they will be judged in media-enhanced ways: your product will have to prove itself in AccelGolf's "digital golf bag," and even those who don't have golf software will hear about the results from those who do. The smart companies will go a step further, reverse-engineering their products to make them appealing parts of the larger multimedia conversation. That might mean, for example, developing clubs that identify themselves by radio signal to your golf app, or balls that can be tracked by GPS, making it easier to measure your performance—and to find balls that get lost. If you offer a service to golf players, you will have to compete with the technological versions of those lessons or advice. Golf may still be golf, but if you are in a golf-related business, you will have to offer products that in some way respond to the sport's media revolution.

Of course, golf on a course is not fully digital. It's not a video game. The point is not that every experience is composed of what we call media to the same degree, it's that there is no percentage in arguing about whether a product "is" or "isn't" media. Every product is somewhere in the middle. (It's easy to forget, but even digitized music files begin with human hands on physical instruments, and human voices emitted from human bodies.) The crucial point is that the "media layers" in even an apparently non-media activity such as golf are not just aspects of marketing or ways of providing background information to players. Over time they change the way the game itself is played—the overall experience. In the C-scape, changes in media alter not just how you sell, but also what you sell.

MEDIA LAYERS ARE NOT OPTIONAL

What if a producer isn't interested in hybrid media experiences? What if a retailer is content with traditional methods or a doctor wants to pay attention to treating patients and not to media technologies? Consider a traditional farmer who only wants to go on bringing produce to the farmer's market. That farmer may be content to keep loading up a truck with arugula and driving it into the city, but his or her customers, the more they want great organic lettuce, are going to want more information about what is available where. If they need sharp, fresh arugula for a salad, they may use WhatIsFresh.com, a website that collects information from greenmarkets and allows users to search by location, day of the week, vendor, and ingredient. If they find they have a choice of greenmarkets, they might use local travel sites for reviews and recommendations. Over time, as more and more producers notice that their customers expect this media-enhanced version of their products—and buy more from those who offer it—every farmer will feel increasing pressure to become a kind of Multimedia Arugula Network, if only on a small scale, perhaps tweeting or blogging about what's on sale that day and printing recipes to distribute in person and on their website.

Similarly, service providers such as doctors will find that not just their addresses and qualifications, and even their rankings (world-class, best in local area, and so on) but also customer ratings of bedside manner, average delay before an appointment in the office, and even the friendliness of their staff are a mouse click away—and that this information creates pressure on their hiring decisions, the amount of time they spend with their patients, and even on the kinds of medications and procedures the patients request. The media layering around the traditional products and services change the products and services themselves.

Journalists had a shock in the years between 2003 and 2007: they discovered that the stories they wrote didn't end when they were printed. They began a new life, layered with media created by others. Readers re-posted the original stories, commented on them, argued with them, linked them to other information that put the story in a new context or even contradicted its main points, and in so doing *remade* the story that journalists had always controlled. Journalists had to learn to see the stories they created in terms of a larger media process that was never in their control. That's where non-media business is now: learning to recognize that products and brands accumulate media layers and become convergent customer experiences, whether producers intended them or not.

As with marketing messages, businesses need to give up dictating what consumers want to do and accept a role more like that of an interested peer. Do consumers value the paper or just the news? The shoe store with its shelves of merchandise and its clerks or just the chance to try on the shoes before they buy? Consumers will use products in unexpected ways, finding value that producers didn't intend; they will expect innovations no one can predict. Only the company that commits to observing how its products are used can discover what business it's actually in.

9

THEY CHOOSE, BUT YOU CURATE

PRODUCT CO-DEVELOPMENT

After decades of success in the toy and game industry, global giant Hasbro was in danger of losing its way. Its first toys had been doctor and nurse kits in the 1940s; the company's first big hit came in 1952 when it bought Mr. Potato Head from an inventor and made it a worldwide sensation. From then on, through G.I. Joe in the 1960s, My Little Pony and Transformers in the 1980s, and movie tie-ins such as Star Wars, its toys were in the hands and imaginations of children around the world. My Little Pony, for a while, even outsold Mattel's Barbie. The company diversified into board games, buying the Milton Bradley Company in 1984 and Parker Brothers in 1991, giving Hasbro control of Monopoly, the most successful board game ever.

Yet even as Hasbro established itself ever more securely in traditional toys and games, their sales in the C-scape began to weaken. Increasingly, young people spent their time immersed in media and entertainment—about half their free time, by Hasbro's current estimates. The only area of the toy industry with strong growth was "where properties and toy lines are being supported by media or entertainment," such as Star Wars tie-ins, as CEO Brian Goldner explained. It wasn't just that kids were buying the toys and games they saw on television and in the movies—that had been true in the 1980s, when the success of My Little Pony rubber figurines grew along with the two television shows and the feature-length movie the toys inspired. The shift went deeper than marketing. Play was changing.

Hasbro was now competing for consumers' attention with companies like Nintendo, the Japanese video game giant that created the role-playing game Pokémon, among others. Children who "played" Pokémon did so in a mind-boggling variety of ways. In a single afternoon, they might play a solo video game, then link their game console to friends' consoles, or interact with players around the world over the Nintendo Wi-Fi Connection. They might watch Pokémon television shows and movies, but also homemade fan videos of "walkthroughs" of difficult portions of games on YouTube. They might clip on a "Pokéwalker" pedometer, to count their steps as they walk and run through the day, earning bonuses within the world of the game. They might read books of Pokémon manga cartoons or study thick guides to plan game strategy, and trade cardboard collectors' cards or use those cards to battle in the Pokémon board game—a paper-and-cardboard pastime that would not have looked much out of place next to the first Mr. Potato Head. They might put on Pokémon costumes and take plastic Poké balls and action figures in hand to act out a story as generations of children have done with dolls and action figures—but now with their play informed by what they had encountered on various screens and in books.

What happened to play here? It was not a simple shift from plastic and cardboard to controller and screen; it was a shift from a small number of choices in a small number of forms to a much greater variety of both. As Hasbro CEO Goldner says, "Young people are particularly adept at seeking out the experiences they want, as they are the most 'digitally native,' and they move between formats of immersion seamlessly and effortlessly. . . . One is not better than the other; they are just different manifestations of brand experiences that the consumer desires."

Just as marketers must realize that the market—the place where commerce happens—is not any given physical location or even any given virtual location, but rather in the convergent relationship with the consumer, Hasbro discovered that play could no longer be confined to traditional spaces. "We cannot and will not relegate our brands to the playroom floor or the kitchen table," Goldner said. And so after more than fifty years as a toy and game manufacturer, "Hasbro is becoming a branded play company."

But how? They could not solve this problem by following the product-development playbook that had brought them success for fifty years. Buying up still more inventive ideas for traditional toys, buying other traditional game makers, or even making toys that tied to other companies' media and entertainment would not keep Hasbro at the forefront of the toy and game industry. Nintendo and other rivals provided a convergent, multimedia play experience wherever and however their young customers wanted it.

So Hasbro moved to develop the capacity to offer consumers the entire convergent play experience. The effort had three parts. Part one was a new movie licensing deal. Building on the success of their original collaboration with Paramount Pictures for the G.I. Joe and Transformers movies, they made a deal with Universal Studios to take longtime board-game brands struggling for consumer relevance in the C-scape—Monopoly, Candyland, Battleship—and produce movies around them. The goal was for the movies to provide not just marketing support for the traditional games, but also a creative infusion, helping the games evolve into more versatile stories. As a board game, Battleship had been a sea battle between two identical, nameless, storyless navies. In the movie, one side became a group of extraterrestrials, bent not on world domination but on satisfying an "ecological interest" in planet Earth that put them in conflict with the other side. Such an approach enriched the play possibilities of the game for the future. A marketing tie-in became a route to product development.

In the second part of Hasbro's attempt to remake itself as a "branded play" company, the company looked for an opportunity in television. Discovery Kids Network had impressive distribution, but the content was lacking. As David Zaslav of Discovery explains, "We recognized that kids programming was not our core competency, so we found a partner in Hasbro who had the expertise and established brands in the kids space that we lacked." Hasbro paid Discovery $300 million to own half of what had been Discovery Kids Network (in the United States). The mission of this new network, called The Hub, was to create shows that were both educational and entertaining, based on Hasbro characters and properties.

Finally, Hasbro also made a deal with Electronic Arts to develop video games around all of these traditional, movie, and video properties. In all of these ways, Hasbro was taking the convergence of play into the company's own hands, with a long-term goal of offering media layers to enhance the experience of playing with hundreds of Hasbro properties and toys.

WHAT EXPERIENCE DO YOUR CUSTOMERS WANT?

What if a business does not have hundreds of millions of dollars to invest in becoming a convergent media conglomerate? Do the principles underlying Hasbro's approach apply to ventures of any size? "Add media layers to expand the customer experience" is too general to be useful. But like the problem of how to decide what marketing messages to send to which market segments, the solution comes back to the four C's.

- What experiences of your product do your consumers choose?
- What kind of content could you provide to support that experience?
- How can you establish yourself as a trustworthy curator of that content?
- And how can you maintain your role as convergence continues to change the landscape?

In the last chapter, I suggested questions to help identify the experience that consumers were *already* having with your brands. Now let's look at ways to build on that knowledge to develop *new* products.

The common mistake many companies make is to try to interest customers in a *new* experience they have never wanted. I think of this mistake as the "Facebook principle." There were, and still are, dozens of social networking sites before Facebook that did everything, technologically, that Facebook did, but they never achieved anything like Facebook's success. Why? They had the goal wrong. They were built around creating a new experience for the user to want, rather than improving an experience the user already wanted. Tribe, Friendster, Meetup, and many other sites all offered the chance to join a community of strangers who shared an interest or a geographical location. Yet few people wake up in the morning and think, "Today, I want to join a group of strangers."

Facebook began with an existing community—college kids—

who knew what experience they were after: they wanted to hook up. They were already doing it, sometimes using the school's traditional printed face book, but it was awkward. A college face book was a book with one small photo of each student in the class and some basic information such as his or her full name, high school, and hometown. It wasn't much, but it was indexed by first name, so you could learn the last name of a student you'd just met, and you could show your friends the person's picture and see if any of them had more information.

Enter Facebook. Now if you met a girl or a guy for the first time, you could go back to your room and look that person up on their Facebook page, find out much more about them, and, if you still felt interested, communicate with them right away through the site. Facebook didn't ask you to join a community of strangers—it reflected a community that already existed. It offered a convergent technology—photos, text, video, one-on-one, and group communication—that made it more convenient to do what you already wanted. You could make contact in a way that was safer than meeting in person and more comfortable than calling on the phone and asking for a date. And as it turned out, millions of people, not just college students looking for romance, wanted that same experience: an easier, faster, less embarrassing way to reconnect with people they already knew but might want to know better.

How can a company improve a consumer experience when consumers don't yet know what they want?

- Look for clues in sales figures. One of the clearest ways consumers speak about the experiences they want is at the cash register. During 2009 online sales through Macys.com for the first time exceeded the sales at the company's flagship store in Manhattan: the 34th Street store that calls itself "the largest store in the world." That fact jolted the Macy's management team into paying more attention to Macys.com, and devoting more resources to growing and improving the online shopping experience.

For Hasbro, sales data made clear that only the toys and games supported by media or entertainment were sustaining growth. However, in Hasbro's case, that "communication by cash register," on its own, might have been misunderstood as a signal that onscreen toys were replacing traditional ones, rather than signaling a larger change in the nature of the play experience and the need to develop the media layers that would sustain convergent play.

- Observe how current products are used—or not used. Another way consumers reveal the product experiences they would prefer is through the ways they fail to use, or misuse, products they already have.

  » All of those VCRs in the 1980s with their clocks flashing "12:00" were a signal that the available product wasn't providing the experience that television watchers wanted. That wanted-but-unrealized experience provided the opportunity for TiVo and other DVRs to replace the VCR.

  » When Coca-Cola observed disappointing sales to teens and moms, it suggested to Coke that those groups weren't finding what they wanted. So Coke redesigned some core products with new packaging. They knew that teens were spending a lot of disposable income on 99-cent music downloads, so Coke introduced a 99-cent, 16-ounce bottle. Moms, meanwhile, were busy and looking for an energy boost, but likely concerned about the calories in soft drinks. For moms, Coke introduced a 90-calorie mini-can. Both new products re-imagined the traditional product in terms of an experience that would fit into their consumers' lifestyles.

» The paper cards cardiologists gave at-risk patients to record their blood pressure at home were often coming back incomplete, or getting lost between doctor visits and not coming back at all. The poor compliance of patients was nothing new, but one group of cardiologists saw the chance to offer patients a better experience of monitoring blood pressure. Those doctors worked with Mobile Commons to develop an alternative. The patients now received text messages on their cell phones, reminding them when it was time to check their blood pressure. Instead of writing the results down, they immediately texted results to a special number, allowing the doctor to have all the data entered on the patients' charts before they came for the next appointment—and a much better sense of whether those home tests had been completed as scheduled. These new-media layers improved the medical experience remarkably.

» Ask consumers directly. Who knows what convergent experiences consumers want? Sometimes, they do.

» Starbucks created a website, "My Starbucks Idea," and invited customers to post ideas for improvements. The suggestions could be anything—from the selection of coffee drinks to packaging, the rewards program, and the company's efforts to strengthen its constituent communities. On the site, customers could vote for the best ideas and check back to see which ideas had been adapted. This approach opened the company up to public criticism—their shift from the "black" to the "gold" reward card system drew extensive complaints, with thousands of votes for scrapping "gold" altogether—but it also gave them access to the creativity of tens of thousands of customers. Discussion on the site led to the creation of new core products such as the Dark Cherry Mocha espresso drink, as well as new aspects of the overall brand, such as photo essays showing how inspectors enforce Starbucks' workplace and environmental standards.

» When Amtrak asked riders what they liked about the then-new Acela Express trains that ran from Boston to New York and Washington, they found women especially giving an unexpected answer: the trains were slow. The train took longer than an airline shuttle, and not only did it take more time, it also passed the time in a slower, less hectic way. Airline passengers had to fight through traffic to the airport, board the plane, get off the plane a short time later, and find their way into the new city. It was not one trip but three, with many interruptions along the way. The train, by contrast, took them from downtown to downtown, and while it did so they could stay in one seat. Working mothers, in particular, loved this aspect: the train was a place where neither coworkers nor family could barge in on them, a chance to be by themselves, in slowness, for a sustained stretch of hours.

These women preferred this more relaxed travel experience, and Amtrak crafted an entire marketing campaign, taking this famous failing of trains compared to airlines and reinventing it as something desirable. Amtrak added electrical outlets to every seat, improved the food choices, and built a follow-up campaign aimed at all business travelers. The campaign appeared on print advertisements; signs and posters; online banner ads; and as a downloadable game for mobile devices called All Aboard. The message throughout this campaign was that Acela trains were a new product, better than ever because they offered what airlines couldn't—big, comfortable seats; lots of legroom; food when you wanted it; power for your devices, and a relaxing experience from "downtown to downtown." The railroad—that old icon of a product that failed to keep up with the times—had found a new niche in the C-scape by reinventing itself as a luxury experience.

CO-CREATE—BUT DON'T GIVE UP CONTROL

Product development becomes truly convergent—and most responsive to consumers' choices about the experiences they want to have—when it goes beyond seeking and implementing customer ideas and enables customer participation in design itself. Makers of everything from computers to cars have succeeded with websites that guide the consumer through a series of choices, offering different components or design touches. Do you want a four-cylinder or a six-cylinder engine in your car? Do you want that computer with an internal or external optical drive? What colors would you prefer? Consumers themselves are taking over some aspects of product design, choosing the specifications of the models they want to buy. Nike has done this with sneakers. Eidia Lush has done it with women's shoes. Boucheron has done it with luxury necklaces, giving the consumer choices about the number and color of gems they would like in some of the company's most famous designs. And 90 percent of car sales involve some exploration of possible features on automaker websites.

The convergences here are wide ranging and powerful, combining advertising, marketing, product development, and sales in a new form of interactive storytelling. The story goes something like this: *Once upon a time I wanted a new car, but I was confused by my choices and afraid I wouldn't find what was truly right for me. So I went on the website and I found help in sorting through the choices and understanding what they might mean to me. It was like being*

paid to watch an ad, because the promise of finding the perfect prod-
uct made it worth my time to look at all the pictures and video and
text the company created to show me. It was like reading a magazine
because I was educated about a product that interests me. It was like
concierge marketing because I was guided to choices that matched my
personal needs. But above all, the company made me a designer for
a day, and piece by piece and choice by choice I built my own dream
purchase. I tried out my options, and when I saw the results onscreen,
I fell in love. That was it! My quest was over. I could see it there, wait-
ing for me. I had to have it.

CONCIERGE PRODUCT DESIGN

Yet as important as this approach is, it represents only the beginning of co-creation in product design, as it still asks the consumer
to do so much. It requires enough background knowledge to make
these design decisions, plus the time and patience to answer a
long series of questions with careful attention. As Yoram Granit,
founder of Israel's Bee TV, puts it, "Who has the nerves to sit and
provide all these answers?" His frustration with long customer surveys informed his development of what might be the more user-
friendly future for co-creating products.

Bee TV is a service designed to improve a familiar, often disappointing experience: locating television programs or movies that
you will enjoy. If you find yourself with time to watch a show or
a movie, and you know you have vast choices available, how do
you choose? With so many options (and more available, it seems,
every day), in the time it would take to review all your choices, you
could miss the chance to watch anything at all. And the point is
that you don't want to spend your leisure time searching; you want
to find the show and watch it.

Bee TV promises a solution to this problem. Granit describes the service not as a search engine but as a "find engine." It selects products that will suit you without requiring you to create a pro-file, describe your preferences, answer multiple-choice questions, or rate the programming you've seen before. It doesn't try to make you explain what you like and why, because those are complex psychological questions that we can't often answer for ourselves. As Granit explained: "I like action movies, but I don't like all action movies. Some of the things I like I would never admit that I like. My perception of myself is not always what I truly am." He could be talking about the consumer of many products or services.

Bee TV's system focuses on something far simpler and more factual: how your television gets used. The approach is based on the idea that even when a television is shared by several people, there are patterns to the way it is used during the day and week and year. The movies shown on a family television on a weekend afternoon, for example, will be different from what is shown after the children are in bed. So the first thing Bee TV does is to ob-serve what kinds of programming are on your television at certain times; when it is turned on again at the same time of day or week, it offers similar choices, providing previews the producer has made available, and even constructing its own previews from publicity material and other sources.

The second thing the system does is to select "similar" pro-gramming in a sophisticated statistical way that goes beyond con-ventional metadata—that is, the tags usually used to identify a program. The movie *Pretty Woman*, for example, might be tagged conventionally by genre (romantic comedy), stars (Julia Rob-erts), story category (a Cinderella-type story), and so on. However, Bee TV doesn't use these conventional categories because no one viewer is going to like every romantic comedy or every Cinderella story. Instead, the computer system goes online to find public places where that movie has been described or discussed. These might include the summaries provided by television networks or news organizations in their listings and reviews, and also discussion boards and other public sites where language is generated about the movie.

The goal is not to do a thoughtful analysis of consumer response or to figure out how best to describe *Pretty Woman*. The goal is to collect what Granit calls a "basket" of language that is analyzed to determine the statistically significant words and phrases associated with this movie. The system then takes these words and locates other programming that has also been described with these same unusual words. "Maybe people tended to use the word 'together' for this movie, near the word 'friendship,'" Granit explained. "Even words like 'although'—statistically, this matrix of content and the results are amazing."

Just as Bee TV avoids having to understand what people like by concentrating on their television usage, it avoids the complex aesthetic questions of how different movies and shows ought to be measured against each other by concentrating not on ideas about shows but on the statistical patterns in the words people use about them—treating online word choice as a quantifiable behavior, just like the behavior of turning on an action movie after the kids go to sleep. Granit is not able to offer any penetrating insights, for example, about the art of cinema or what made *Pretty Woman* so popular. Even if you looked at the words his system collected to tag a particular movie, they wouldn't make any conventional sense. But he is not in the business of understanding culture. He is in the business of tailoring consumers' experiences of television.

In addition to observing user behavior and crowdsourcing metadata about programs, Bee TV also attempts to track larger cultural trends in what makes desirable programming. Certain events make some kinds of shows more immediately appealing to viewers—the Christmas season, for example, changes what people want to watch in reliable ways, ways that go beyond fare with an explicit holiday theme. The death of an actor or other well-known figure makes programming that features that person more compelling. Certain news events create interest in programming about those topics or themes—the anniversary of the fall of the Berlin Wall might prompt an interest in thrillers set behind the Iron Curtain. So far, Bee TV has not developed an automatic way to track these trends, so they exercise a human, editorial influence, pushing relevant trends.

Bee TV is not in the product development business. What they have created is a system for marketing existing products (movies and television programs), not a model for designing new ones. But there is no reason that the same approach could not become part of the development process for any product that consumers buy repeatedly. Your life history of restaurant-going, for example, could be analyzed in terms of statistical patterns in the language other people use online to describe restaurant experiences, and cross-referenced with restaurants in your area. Such information might not only help you find more restaurants to your taste, it could help investors determine if there is a market for a certain style of restaurant in your area, and help restaurateurs decide if their latest idea is worth a shot.

The best that an approach like this could do for a product development team might be to determine the comparative levels of interest in a population of consumers for one of several design prototypes. But that could be enough. There will still be designers—and consumers themselves—to suggest ideas and develop prototypes. But an approach like Bee TV might take some of the work out of curating those new designs—deciding what to offer whom.

EVERY COMPANY IS AN EXPERIENCE CURATOR

Now that what matters about a product is increasingly the media-informed customer experience that develops around it, a product design team needs to think of itself in part as a group of curators, offering consumers choices of experiences. They need to provide both the core products and the surrounding media layers. While the spotlight these days is on the consumer, the producer still maintains an essential editorial role.

"My Starbucks Idea" might sound at first as if the company is handing over control to its customers, but Starbucks remains selective about which ideas are developed and how they are developed. The ideas that customers propose and vote on are directed to individual Starbucks employees, who help shape them into practical additions to the Starbucks product experience and then present them back to their customers on the website. It's a brilliant fit, because the employees tend to have both a deep understanding of the company (they work there) and their own personal experience of the Starbucks brand (they eat and drink there). They are natural ambassadors, brokering compromises between company and consumer. Customers get the pleasure of a personalized response from inside the company, but while the ideas may be the customers', the company retains control.

Why is such control necessary in the age of "crowdsourcing" and "user-generated content" and brands that "belong to the consumer"? Although consumers have important creative contributions to make, they are not good at overall product design. I hear this sentiment across the spectrum of business, from traditional to new-media cutting edge. John Makinson, CEO of Penguin Books, an innovator of multimedia textbooks on multiple platforms, told me about his company's experiment at crowdsourcing the writing of a "wiki-novel" called *A Million Penguins.* "Tens of thousands of people engaged in that project," he said. "And we would take it down every night and try and edit it and remove the obscenities and all the references to bananas and try to knock it into shape. [But] they didn't improve it, actually. It ended up even worse, I think, than it started."

Yoram Granit put it even more starkly, explaining why Bee TV would not include user-posted YouTube video. "We call [purely] user-generated content *loser*-generated content." Similarly, advertising guru Jon Bond described for me why even though some individual advertisements created by consumers can be excellent, professional agencies are still necessary to create and manage overall campaigns: "In truth, the consumer isn't very good at it. Making insightful, sustainable, effective long-term campaigns is a skill that no amateurs possess, and frankly more than a few of us professionals often struggle with it as well. . . . So now what? If total control is old school, and tabula rasa results in unwatchable crap, is there a happy medium?"

He offered as a possible answer the example of an ad campaign in Europe that took the form of a soap opera. "They solicit script ideas from consumers for their ongoing soap opera type campaign (an easy format to work from, without Shakespearean standards). They take the best ideas and get professional writers, directors, and producers to work on it. And the result is something actually good. Everyone wins. That's co-creation. The skill in co-creation is leaving enough room for the consumer to contribute something meaningful, but also providing enough support so that the end product comes out well."

It's a balance that remains difficult for most companies to get right. Traditional companies still resist letting go of any control of their hard-earned brands—and perhaps Granit will find that some user-generated content is worth including in his system. On the other hand, companies created in the digital revolution tend to overvalue the contributions users make, not recognizing the need to guide content creation and in the end, control the brand. But while the biases on both sides are ingrained, the underlying steps are simple:

1. Give consumers limited areas where they can make creative contributions.
2. Turn those contributions over to your professional design team, and have them create prototypes or alternatives based on customer ideas.
3. Give consumers choices of new products or approaches, seeking evaluations and feedback, or perhaps automating some of that process, one day, along the lines of Bee TV's data collection.

And so the convergent wheel turns. In the C-scape, to make the crucial choices about which products get developed as part of what longer-term strategy, and who serves in which development roles, consumers choose, but companies continue to curate.

10

LOYALTY THAT LASTS

PRODUCT EXPERIENCES THAT EVOLVE
WITH THE C-SCAPE

How does a company keep a customer loyal? Not so long ago, a company could win a customer in a number of different ways, and content wasn't necessarily the most important. Consider the bland, inauthentic versions of "Italian" or "Chinese" or "Mexican" foods that for years were all many consumers could find on their supermarket shelves. Although other companies might have made better-tasting, more authentic, cheaper ethnic food products, if one company had better marketing and a national distribution deal with the major supermarket chains, the power of its monopoly or near-monopoly could trump quality and price. In the C-scape, however, not even high-tech marketing beats content. As Arnaud Deschamps of Nespresso told me: "You can't compensate with communication for your lack of product. The product has to sell itself."

It would seem that there are two strong strategies left: treat a product as a commodity, the same as what the competition produces, and offer it for the lowest price; or offer some uniquely better form of the product, a higher-quality experience. What seems certain is that in the C-scape, if what one sells is in the middle—middling quality, moderate price—a company is in trouble. CDs were not as thrilling as live concerts but not as cheap and convenient as MP3 files. They got lost between the two strategies and died there. I agree with what journalist Kevin Maney calls the "fidelity swap." As described in his book *Trade-Off,* "The most successful products and services tend to be either high in fidelity or high in convenience—one or the other, but not both. In fact, products attempting to be both typically end up with a confused brand. Imagine McDonald's trying its hand at gourmet meals."

I am not convinced, though, that there are even two workable strategies left. Treating a product as a commodity—assuming that what a company sells is no different from what the competition sells—and working to offer the lowest-priced option isn't going to sustain a company in the long term. Of course, there will always be some company whose product is cheapest, and that company will find buyers. The basic laws of supply and demand won't change. But in the C-scape, there are two reasons why I think treating products as commodities is a losing strategy for any given company over time.

First, the barriers to entry in the C-scape are so much lower, and competition is so much more intense, that I doubt if anyone can hang on as the lowest-cost provider for long. Electronics discount stores like Crazy Eddie were driven out of business by megastores like The Good Guys and Circuit City, many of which have lost out to Internet-based stores that don't have the overhead of brick-and-mortar operations. And now there is Invisible Hand, a web-browser application that recognizes when a user is shopping at an online store and automatically searches for lower prices. There are just too many innovations coming from all directions, and chances are that a competitor with less overhead will find a way to come in with a lower price.

Second, because consumers have so much more information easily available to them, essentially for free, they can discover variations in products that they might once have accepted as identical. Consider differences in taste between generic brands of cough syrup. In the past, the buyer of the lowest-priced cough syrup might have put up with an odd taste if the remedy worked, if it fit his or her budget, and if finding an alternative seemed inconvenient. (What would you have had to do? Travel from one chain store to the next, buy a bottle of each generic cough syrup in town, and conduct a taste test?)

Now, though, a person can query friends or social networks— "Did anyone else notice that No-Brand Cough-n-Cold tastes funny?"—and find an alternative generic brand at another chain store at the same price. No-Brand's attempt to be the low-priced product has lost out to a competitor who provides a better overall experience. Perhaps a customer would even pay a little more for that alternative—if so, then even at the low price point the crucial factor is still the quality of the experience.

I find Maney's example of McDonald's in comparison to a gourmet restaurant misleading, as a Big Mac and a gourmet meal, while both dinners, are not comparable consumer experiences. (No one heads out to McDonald's, sees that it's too crowded, and picks a Michelin-rated restaurant instead.) McDonald's has made an enormous effort to build a brand around a reliable style of food, service, and decor: you'll find the same familiar food served in the same familiar way around the world, which some consumers find reassuring and satisfying. The point, always, is that only the consumer decides what counts as quality.

For both of those reasons—the difficulty of keeping the position as the low-cost provider and the difficulty of forcing well-informed consumers with plenty of choices to accept that products are commodities—the only approach to product development that will last in the C-scape is to offer consumers a distinctive quality product.

KEEP IT NEW

Designing and marketing such a product is only the beginning; it's necessary to keep it relevant, giving consumers new reasons to keep choosing it, purchase after purchase.

Retailing legend Millard "Micky" Drexler faced this conundrum when he took over as CEO of J. Crew. The clothing brand was considered out of touch with contemporary tastes and speed. What could turn it around? Drexler knew that J. Crew had to provide high-quality, creative products, but he also knew that wouldn't be enough. "The speed at which things change has never been faster," he said, "and your franchise only lasts as long as the product remains on target." He decided to break the old rules of fashion and serve the consumer's desire not just for a compelling brand experience but for an ongoing series of interesting experiences. To do so, he rewrote the fashion calendar. Rather than offering new product designs every sixteen weeks, perhaps every twelve weeks, as had been traditional in an industry that offered new lines for each new "season," J. Crew began to offer a new "season" every seven weeks. In effect, they made time in the fashion world move twice as fast. The more-frequent arrival of original, high-quality products recaptured consumers' attention, and J. Crew, which once seemed to be dying, reestablished itself.

James Fielding, president of the Disney Store retail chain, had a similar experience. Even during hard economic times, he found, when Disney introduced new products that were not available elsewhere, his customers responded to innovation and quality even more than to price. Explaining his success during a recessionary holiday season, he explained, "We were smart in our pricing, but we led with quality and newness."

But while it is fairly simple for a retailer to make a decision to offer a greater variety of products for sale more often, what are the alternatives for businesses that lack a retailer's near-endless variety of new products to select from? What if your business is known for only a single brand? And how do you keep improving a product that has already made its name by claiming to be the best?

The Swiss company Nespresso learned to see what it sold not as a single product (espresso coffee), nor even as a range of different flavors of that product (a menu for a coffee experience), but as an evolving series of experiences. To provide customers with more elements of that widening experience, the company gradually broadened its offerings from the elements necessary to prepare coffee (coffee makers and coffee capsules) to the cups and saucers and other aspects of preparation and service: spoons, milk frothers, sugar sticks, serving trays, decorative stands on which to store and display the colorful coffee capsules, and so forth. Of course, there was nothing remarkable about a company offering a range of related products as a way to increase its revenue streams. But the crucial addition here was the way these products refreshed the consumer's experience.

Recognizing that many of their customers eat chocolate when they drink coffee, the company introduced "chocolate bites," a line of ten kinds of chocolate. Nespresso didn't claim that they could now make the best chocolate in the world—that would have been introducing an entirely new product. Instead, they offered chocolates that were, they said, the best designed to complement and harmonize with their blends of coffee. On their website and in the coffee boutiques, customers could learn, for example, to pair a coffee with some bitterness and a chocolate with some acidity, or to harmonize the "cereal notes" in both, just as they might also pair wines with foods. For customers who enjoyed this "connoisseur" approach to coffee, the product became new again, just as a fresh "season" at J. Crew made the catalog or store seem newly compelling, giving customers a reason to come back.

If the key for companies seeking to maintain customer loyalty is to keep refreshing the product experience they offer, then success depends on knowing not just what customers want now, but what they might prefer in the future. One might say that in the C-scape, *every* company is in the *same* business—gathering and understanding data on evolving customer habits and preferences. As Yoram Granit of Bee TV told me, he doesn't know how his customers will access television shows and movies in a few years, whether from television stations or from studios distributing over the Internet. He doesn't know which of the means of receiving video programming will last—there are now over 250 ways, ranging from phones to videogame consoles. But he feels confident that he will still have a business as long as he continues to gather information about what kind of programming each individual customer watches. "Our holy grail," he said, "is actually the data that we're collecting for the viewers." As long as his data on customer preferences keeps improving, he can continue to offer a unique and increasingly sophisticated consumer experience. That ever-improving experience is what makes customers stay loyal.

Apple is one of the best examples of a company that has kept a laser focus on reinventing products to provide an evolving customer experience, yet its success is often misunderstood. As a cover editorial in the *Economist* put it, "Rather than developing entirely new product categories, [Apple] excels at taking existing, half-baked ideas and showing the rest of the world how to do them properly." That's true, but what is so "proper" about the way Apple does it? What they offer is not simply technological innovation—before the Macintosh appeared in 1984, there were other mouse-based personal computers with graphical interfaces; before the iPod, other small digital-music players; before the iPhone, other smartphones; before the iPad, other tablet computers—including Apple's own flop, the Newton. Why did the Apple versions of these existing ideas achieve such success and inspire such intense loyalty?

They addressed all four C's. In terms of the first C, consumer choice, Apple has been exceptional at discovering what consumers consider ease and convenience, and then building that into the product experience. I remember the first time I saw a Macintosh computer come out of the box: there were no wires! Usually, with a personal computer, you began by laying out the pieces and cords on the floor, and then hooking them together following a diagram that might not have been drawn with the understanding that the main processor was going to sit on the floor while the monitor would be tucked in among bookshelves. One's first impression of a new desktop PC often involved frustration and delay, but the Macintosh was one-piece and wireless. It was years before PC manufacturers offered one-piece computers or even redesigned their wires with color connectors that could be matched at each end, between the computer, screen, keyboard, and mouse.

With the introduction of iTunes, Apple was the first company to recognize that part of what they were selling was an improved consumer experience of paying for songs. Apple priced all songs at ninety-nine cents, an artificially low price with no relationship to demand (now no longer standard), that helped overcome resistance to buying music among users used to free, illegal downloads. Yet while that approach now seems ordinary, at the time their competitors' companies didn't want to touch it. Credit-card companies charged retailers a minimum fee per transaction—often twenty-five cents, which represented a huge piece of each ninety-nine-cent sale. For that reason, "everyone knew" that you couldn't sell individual songs and accept payment by credit card, however convenient that might be for the buyer.

Apple decided to delay accepting payment for its smallest orders, waiting until it could bundle them together and only pay the credit card company one "minimum" fee for the bundled transaction. Many consumers were unaware of the change Apple had made, but now the company could offer a convenience no one had thought possible—you could make an impulse purchase of less than a dollar and bill it to a credit card already on file. And notice Apple's priorities: first they designed an appealing customer payment experience, and then they innovated to make it economically viable.

In terms of the second C, Apple has shown its understanding that the "content" isn't just the device it sells. The "content" is the full customer experience. While they didn't make the first smartphone, they made the first one with an intuitive, graphics-based interface that didn't require pecking out a lot of letters on a tiny keyboard. Similarly, among the many MP3 players already crowding the field when Apple released the iPod, not one came with a software package that made it easy for the consumer to download and manage music from a central store, as the iTunes software did.

The iTunes software also addressed the third C, curation, with its "Genius" feature, which makes recommendations for further listening and viewing based on what a customer has already purchased. It provides this guidance for both content the customer already owns and content the customer might choose to buy.

Yet Apple is sometimes criticized in the new-media world for not being forward-thinking enough. As writer Michael Wolff put it, "[Apple founder and CEO Steve] Jobs has stubbornly—or fetishistically—bucked one of the most fundamental trends in technology and information, that the future is not hardware (it hasn't been for three generations), it's software." In this view, Apple is "failing" to abide by the new-media rules that hold hardware to be out and software in. But to my mind, Apple has instead recognized the fourth C: that in convergence, new doesn't replace old; it combines the two and creates an unfolding series of new hybrids. Hardware and software have converged: software that can't run on a device that fits in your pocket, for example, is no use to a consumer on the go, no matter what it does.

Similarly, a larger screen as on the iPad makes the basic iTunes software appealing for new categories of content—magazines, newspapers, textbooks, video novels, video games, and even videos themselves. Apple has been wise to continue as both a hardware and a software innovator—for software, the App Store makes Apple's products endlessly customizable, offering a convergent consumer experience that evolves new possibilities by the day. Both hardware and software still matter when it comes to offering consumers the greatest possible choice—and for that reason, every company must keep an eye on changes in technology that connects it to its customers, because the impact of that technology can remake the marketplace. It is not enough for Bee TV to know exactly what a consumer would like to see if they aren't prepared to deliver that show on the hardware and software the consumer wants. It is not enough for J. Crew to speed up the "seasons" and offer more variety more often if it doesn't also find the combinations of hardware and software that display the company's offerings and make shopping easy. The catalog that looks amazing on a laptop may not have any visual appeal on a smartphone. Disney is not only emphasizing new products, but developing what it hopes will be a new experience of shopping, a makeover priced at a million dollars per store. As reported in the *New York Times*, "Computer chips embedded in packaging will activate hidden features. Walk by a 'magic mirror' while holding a Princess tiara, for instance, and Cinderella might appear and say something to you. . . .

If a clip from Disney's coming 'A Christmas Carol' is playing in the theater, the whole store might suddenly be made to smell like a Christmas tree." As Fielding told the *Hub Magazine,* the televisions that will show content in the store are "100 percent proprietary to us [and] deliver content in a way that has never been seen before." Customer loyalty depends not only on the quality of the evolving product experience but also on the evolving quality of the hardware and software media that communicate it.

I'm a longtime cell phone customer. Why shouldn't I switch to the latest new phone with the newest operating system? Why should I stick with Sprint or AT&T or Verizon when I've got lots of choices and plenty of good information? I've got a contract with you, but it will expire. I've got your equipment, but I'll need to replace it, and anyway, you have no lock on technological innovation. I've got my data with you, but increasingly it is stored on the Internet; with some effort, that data is portable. I've had good experiences with your brand in the past, I may have an emotional connection, and I receive your marketing messages and your helpful information, but you're not the only one sending me useful and compelling messages. All of those reasons give me *some* motivation to stay loyal, but none of them locks me in like the old monopoly arrangements used to do. Meanwhile I've got a wandering eye and a hunger for newness. But if you combine all of those partial motivations with a convincing promise, regularly fulfilled, I may just accept dependence on you to provide that evolving experience— and stay loyal, even in the C-scape.

PART FOUR

WHAT HAPPENS TO BUSINESSES?

11

PRICE THE EXPERIENCE, NOT THE PRODUCT

NEW APPROACHES TO REVENUE

There is a story being told these days by many in media, ranging from journalists and authors to television and music industry executives to software designers and pornographers—in fact, from makers of every form of media that can be shared digitally. It's a story that strikes fear into the heart of anyone with a product that can be sold or resold online—or at least, it should inspire serious concern, if it's true. The story goes like this: once upon a time, consumers respected content and the people who made it; they paid a fair price based on its value, and in so doing they generated the revenue streams that made great content possible. But now, the story continues, we live in dark days. People no longer value great reporting or creative work or intellectual property, and for that reason these cultural forms and their creators can no longer generate enough revenue to support themselves. They are doomed to wither and die.

The evidence usually cited is the now-familiar decline of journalism and the music industry, yet a closer look at the evidence tells a different story. While revenue in these industries has declined sharply, consumer spending in these general areas has not. Readership of magazines has remained strong. As David Carey, a magazine group president at Condé Nast, told me, "Raw consumer demand as measured by subscription rates has not changed." Similarly, while music industry revenue has fallen, overall music-related spending, including concerts and merchandise not traditionally sold by record companies, has held steady. Consumers will still pay for what they want.

When it comes to monetization—how to turn content into revenue—too many of us still ask the wrong question. We shouldn't be asking how to get back to some imaginary good old days in which consumers rationally and respectfully paid for content. Revenue was never that logical or transparent. The right question is how, in the C-scape, do we improvise creative new arrangements that will work well enough to support all the constituents of content?

The C-scape has changed both the old rules and the new possibilities for revenue. Let's begin with pricing. Prices for almost everything were once far less settled than we now expect. Before the supermarket and the department store, a consumer could often find many small merchants in the market, downtown, or traveling from town to town. With each one, there was a chance for a negotiation over price based on a personal interaction and sometimes an ongoing private relationship. But just as the new-media technologies of the twentieth century were in some ways steps *backward* for the consumer, offering fewer choices, less power, and greater social isolation compared to what came before them—think of someone alone with the television years ago, choosing from among just a few local stations—so too twentieth-century pricing limited and standardized a negotiation that was once far more personal and varied. Large stores tended to establish at least local monopolies on what they offered and how they priced it, and that gave them the power to refuse to bargain. They might discount during sale periods, or as a technique to drive smaller competitors out of business, but the stores scheduled those sales as they chose.

In the C-scape, however, as consumers have gained greater power to shop where and when they want, and with better information about pricing across the country and around the world, sellers are finding that once-settled deals around prices must be renegotiated. Consumers are reclaiming lost powers (to bargain, and to shop peer-to-peer on secondary markets such as Craigslist and eBay) and discovering new powers they never imagined. As airlines have discovered, not only can consumers find every available price offered by any airline for a flight on a given day with one web search, they can get instant, computerized recommendations about whether to buy at today's prices or wait, based on statistical analysis of the airlines' past price-setting behavior.

THE DECLINE OF TRADITIONAL REVENUE

The immediate effect of increased consumer power over price was to cut revenue. In industry after industry, the dramatic impact of increased competition dampened earnings. Hotel rooms could be purchased from one source at less than half the price of another source. Consumer electronics prices plummeted because of the availability of comparison prices and subsequent purchase of anything on the Internet. Pharmaceutical companies found customers ordering generic versions of their products from foreign factories. Even the price of some luxury goods dropped as they became more easily available on discount sites.

The question is how to monetize content in the changed world of the C-scape. If traditional approaches to pricing and revenue are endangering the businesses that rely on them, what are the alternatives?

"I think we've figured it out," Julie Greenwald, the president of Atlantic Records, told the *New York Times*. "It used to be that you could connect five dots and sell a million records. Now there are 20 dots you can connect to sell a million records." What are all those new dots that Atlantic connects? New, smaller revenue streams such as ring tones, satellite radio, iTunes sales, and subscription services, among others. These are different ways for a consumer to hear and use music, many of which can overlap—the same customer may want to hear a given artist on an MP3 player, an online radio station, and as a ringtone—and so that company can collect revenue on the same music multiple times. Atlantic has coordinated these many smaller products based on consumer choice: recognizing the varied places, times, and ways that people now want recorded music in their lives, and offering as many as possible. These offerings served both as their own sources of revenue and as marketing support for the traditional product, the album. "Today you have to be like Leonard Bernstein," chairman and CEO Craig Kallman said, "making sure everyone [in the marketing effort] is hitting the right notes at just the right millisecond." Carefully orchestrated, these new revenue streams led Atlantic to an industry first: more than half of its revenue came from digital sales. And not only did their approach improve sales of digital products, it also slowed the decline of traditional sales such as compact discs.

CONCIERGE PRICING

It's not just that companies need to offer more products for sale to increase their revenue streams. A price, like a marketing message or a product design, is part of the overall consumer experience—and that experience, not the product alone, is what consumers value. Pricing must be "designed" as creatively as products or advertisements, and with as much respect for the role of the consumer.

Yet many industries remain stuck, as magazines have been, in a mass-market model of pricing, based on the authority of the producer and the assumed passivity of the consumer. In that traditional model, which you would find in a traditional supermarket or department store or catalog, the seller offers one or a small number of pricing choices and the consumer must take them or leave them. Magazines, for example, traditionally could be bought at the newsstand or by subscription. A subscription was inexpensive and offered perhaps two choices: one-year or two-year. Those inexpensive subscriptions did one thing well: convince "entry level" consumers to take the risk. That was a good way to increase the subscriber base, which was important when advertising paid for most of the magazine and advertisers wanted to attract as many eyeballs as possible. But in the C-scape, when advertising is paying for a lower percentage of content and eyeballs alone won't make an ad campaign succeed, this pricing structure has become harder to sustain—and it doesn't serve either companies or consumers as well.

David Carey of Condé Nast pointed to his own personal experience of magazines as an example. Some publications are so essential to the way he does his job that he subscribes to both the print and the online versions, and as soon as they arrive, he not only reads them, he forwards urgent news and insight from them to friends and colleagues. He's happy to pay $250 for the subscription to a magazine that covers his industry, such as *AdAge*. "But I love it so much, and it's so important to my job as a thinking person in the business world, that if they had a thousand-dollar product I would buy it," he says. In fact, if he could pay $3,000 a year and get it on Friday, while regular subscribers had to wait until Monday, he would.

From my point of view, Carey was describing what we could call the potential for concierge pricing, in which product design and "pricing design" are united to create alternative experiences for customers at different price points. Sometimes it's a question of offering the same product but in an exclusive, luxury version. Many record companies now offer a deluxe boxed set of an album in a limited edition, pressed on vinyl, with exclusive photographs, commentary, and other bonus materials, for ten times the cost of a basic MP3 album download.

Similarly, JetBlue Airlines, which during its first ten years had been known for simple pricing models, began to offer seats with more legroom for more money. Now, when you go online to get your reservation, you are asked if you want a seat in the exit row or in the first several rows of the plane (which have additional space) for an additional fee, anywhere from $15 to $40.

In search of creative pricing, companies may need to venture beyond tweaking a product, as JetBlue has done, and go far beyond the product it has offered before. Carey believes the future of revenue for the magazine industry may depend in part on building "membership clubs" that offer the most loyal and affluent readers of key print brands a much deeper experience than a traditional magazine can provide. He described a loyalty program Condé

Nast is considering for *Golf Digest* magazine, inspired by the "platinum card" offered by American Express. "We need the ability to hyper-price segments," Carey told me. "If you buy a car, you can buy super-deluxe or basic. At a hotel you can stay in a suite with a view of the ocean or in an ordinary room facing the hills. . . . So what can we do for the $500 subscriber that the $15 customer doesn't get?"

In the proposed "titanium" subscription plan, members would get exclusive content not part of the regular magazine, and an exclusive year-end book on the year in golf, assembled by the magazine's staff. They would have the chance to see and even test new equipment when the magazine received it, before it was available to the public; to walk courses with a *Golf Digest* editor; and to attend special golf meet-and-greets. The company would take a concierge approach to both product and pricing design, going far beyond the traditional question of how to sell magazines. Their "titanium" subscription would be a subscription not just to a magazine but to a year of immersion in the golf world and the golf lifestyle—that is, a subscription to the experience that drew magazine readers in the first place. *Golf Digest* would no longer be just a simple publication. It could also be a golf-experience concierge service, with a price to match.

The logic here is the 80–20 rule applied to pricing: for almost any product or service, there are many casual users, a smaller number of "power" users who will pay a premium, and a tiny fraction of even more devoted users. Carey speculated that there were probably a few *Vogue* fans so devoted to fashion that they would pay to travel with the magazine's editors to Milan for the fashion shows, even if it cost, say, $75,000 for the privilege. They might become something like theater producers, who help to fund productions in exchange for active involvement with the show as it develops.

To take advantage of concierge pricing, however, companies will have to overcome the traditional fear that selling to one customer at a discount will undercut the price that others will be willing to pay. Imagine a hotel with a capacity of one hundred rooms that finds it can rent only 50 or 60 percent for a given season. To rent more, they advertise a buy-one-get-one-free sale in a variety of media. That kind of discounting will rent the excess inventory, but it has costs. The first cost is the money spent on advertising. The second is the feeling among customers who paid full price that their experience is tarnished.

To avoid these results, companies traditionally offered few price points and hid the differences as much as they could. One common approach for European brands has been parallel distribution: selling overstock through unofficial networks in Asia or Latin America. The brands knew their merchandise would come back through gray-market dealers and sometimes claimed to be the victims of unscrupulous resellers even while negotiating price levels with those resellers in private.

A somewhat similar approach is common in the United States with packaged goods of many kinds. A brand will often take a product made at one factory and sell some as its main brand and some as a generic "house brand." The only differences are the label, the price, and the stores that carry the product. Clothing companies will make clothes under their own brand and that of a retail store, which might even sell both.

In the C-scape, however, both the need for this secretive approach and its effectiveness have broken down. There are two reasons for this change, one bad for brands and one good. First, greater access to information means that shipping overstock to foreign countries no longer hides the cheaper prices from domestic buyers. Second, the media revolution has made it far easier and less expensive to create alternative sales arrangements. Online, any company can create as many virtual stores as it needs, each with its own unique offerings.

Jacques-Antoine Granjon has done just that with the French online discounter Vente-privee. When a brand comes to him with excess inventory of whatever kind—he has sold designer clothing, jewelry, hotel rooms, watches, cars, apartments, concert tickets, and more—he arranges a brief online sale at a high discount, often 70 percent off, available only through his website. His staff of 1,200 creates online catalogs and advertising, including video, which are seen by a million visitors per day. Their email notices go out to a list of over 8 million registered members. His peak sales time is between 7:00 and 8:00 in the morning. The company sold 18 million pieces of merchandise in 2008 alone. "I have two hundred thousand people trying to buy on a Monday—a cloudy, cold morning—because I have discounts they can find no place else," he says.

Why don't Vente-privee's discount offerings undercut the brands' own full-price sales? Because the overall consumer experiences are separate, in at least three ways. First, Vente-privee's offerings are set apart in time. Granjon offers only what he calls "leftovers," items already offered at full price and now beyond the point where they can earn the company's traditional profit margin. For some customers, the fact that the merchandise is not new changes the experience entirely—they don't want just any Chanel, they want only this season's Chanel, and what Vente-privee sells is too old. Second, the sales are set apart in space—the sale takes place only on the website, not in the places where shoppers would be offered full-price merchandise. The only place to see the discounted prices for individual items is on their site. That means customers who paid full price are much less likely to learn about the discounts on specific items. Third, and perhaps most important, Vente-privee's sales are inconvenient. They are brief, and you have to wake up early to catch the best of them. The shopping experience (in pajamas, say, trying not to spill your morning coffee on your laptop) is nothing like being waited on at a full-service boutique.

For all those reasons, even if customers find a familiar brand at a Vente-privee sale, they can't develop the same kind of relationship with Vente-privee that they could have with the primary brand. If a consumer, for example, goes into Naf Naf or Banana Republic looking for a sweater, she expects that the brand has done everything possible to have the color and the size she wants—they produce excess inventory so they don't have to tell any customer "no"; they send for inventory from other stores if they are out of her size; they apologize for any delay or disappointment; and so forth. By contrast, Vente-privee stocks only what it has, and even if a customer finds a certain item of clothing or a hotel room at a great discount today, there's no reason to think she'll be able to find anything like it at that price in the future. As a customer experience, it is unreliable and unpredictable—and offers no loyalty at all. Yet that unpredictability itself makes it satisfying for those customers who want a less reliable, more exciting shopping experience.

Companies can maximize revenue by offering their products as part of different shopping experiences, differently priced for different customers. At Boucheron, Bedos analyzed the patterns of its sales and found that among customers who paid full price in its stores, those who bought at the company's carefully designed "friends and family sales," and those who bought overstock through discounters such as Vente-privee, there was little overlap.

Brands, he concluded, should learn to "supply their products for different consumer groups."

THE POWER OF THE SUBSCRIPTION MODEL

Another way to maintain revenue by varying the "pricing experience" is to sell subscriptions, or subscription-like relationships. While revenue for sales of individual items has decreased in the C-scape, the subscription model has proved resilient. Even in the recession of 2008, consumers did not cancel their cell phone subscriptions, cable television subscriptions, or movie rental subscriptions services, though this was widely predicted. The success of the subscription model is partly due to the psychological satisfactions it offers. For example, the American Express "platinum card" and other credit card "membership" programs have been successful even though the services offered are utilized at a low rate— apparently members like the pleasure and reassurance of knowing the services are there, just in case. Perhaps they are like the buyer of an all-expense-paid vacation who spends the entire week ignoring his athletic and entertainment choices and instead lies on a beach chair all day. Part of the pleasure is the awareness that it's all waiting for you if you want it, and part of it is taking a break from mental budgeting.

In a sense, any long-term relationship with a brand is a form of subscription, or it can be if the company designs the product and the pricing structure to encourage it. If I'm loyal to a certain model of car, in effect I pay the company a fairly regular fee (the price of each new car and regular service fees) and receive in return a bundle of features, some of which I didn't know I would get and some of which I will never use. Some stockbrokers have revised their models to offer flat-rate fees to active traders; banks give better rates in exchange for maintaining a minimum balance in accounts; ice cream parlors, cafés, grocery stores, and drugstores have frequent-user cards that reward subscriber-like loyalty. Carefully managed, the consistent (if not always regular) transactions become a comfortable habit.

BEYOND NEW PRODUCTS AND NEW PRICING: REVENUE SHARING

To go even further with innovative pricing, companies must learn to focus on pricing not just their products but the value their products create for others. Here again, the magazine industry, under intense pressure, is innovating in ways that can benefit almost any business. David Carey gave the example of *Condé Nast Traveler,* which often designates five travel agents as experts on a given itinerary and provides their contact information. As a result, those travel agents may receive $20 million to $30 million in bookings from customers whose trips are, in effect, curated by the magazine—but until recently, Condé Nast hasn't shared in that revenue. As Carey put it, "The problem is, we're inspiring the consumption, but then we walk away from it because we don't want to seem conflicted. Meanwhile publications are going out of business."

Just as search engines have broken down the traditional wall been journalism and marketing, so too they have broken down the wall between journalism and direct sales. It's not just that people will cut out an itinerary from a magazine and hand it to a travel agent. A single web search will bring up both the travel information and offers for plane tickets and hotels. This change inspired the creation of the *Wall Street Journal*'s travel agency, WSJTravel, which promises trips around the world for "any range of budget" and destinations "inspired by articles" from the newspaper. "Just as you have come to rely on *The Wall Street Journal's* perspective on global events, many WSJtravel vacations will let you experience a destination from a completely new viewpoint," the announcement said. The *Journal* and the *New York Times* have also launched wine clubs to share in the revenue from consumption inspired by their wine critics.

But in the C-scape, consumers increasingly get the information they trust not just from traditional journalistic sources but from company websites, company blogs, and company social media pages: in a sense, every company is now in the service journalism business. That means every company has the same opportunities to share in the revenue that Carey sees for newspapers and magazines. Johnson & Johnson draws many users to its website on the strength of its well-known brand. An expectant mother might find a link there to the company's BabyCenter website, where she can post information about herself, learn about pregnancy, and interact with other pregnant women and new mothers. If she clicks on the choice to join a group specifically for women expecting in a certain month, she may see an ad for The Baby Registry by Diapers.com, where she can register for baby shower gifts. If she fills out the registry, she will be offered lists of recommended products. Even if the products she registers for are not Johnson & Johnson products, the company can still receive payment for the referral when she clicks on the link to the Diapers.com site; this is known as cost-per-click or cost-per-acquisition advertising. In this seemly and indirect manner, Johnson & Johnson uses its brand to inspire consumption of other brands' products, and shares in the revenue that results by creating a hub-and-spoke arrangement of websites, with the main website as the central hub, free of any advertising for outside brands, and the spokes as secondary websites that feature cost-per-click ads.

DIVERSIFY REVENUE STREAMS

When I founded MarketWatch, we began by offering our financial news for individual amateur investors for free, and we built a huge audience. However, we were dependent on advertising revenue, and I was uncomfortable with relying solely on advertising for the long term. I knew from my newspaper days how advertising revenues can fluctuate with the economy, so I looked for other revenue streams we could build. After we went public and our stock price was high, we used stock to acquire companies with different revenue models. One, Big Charts, built web-based tools to analyze stocks and track their performance, to better identify investment opportunities. A second, the *Hulbert Financial Digest*, sold a subscription-based newsletter that helped evaluate the performance of investment newsletters.

We began licensing some of the products from these businesses to other sites, which proved fortunate when the Internet bubble burst in 2001 and our advertising revenue fell by half. We also started licensing the content we created—financial news—to brokerage sites. It was still free (and generating ad revenue) on our site, but brokerage sites wanted our information on their own sites, too. Stock market news, it seemed, was one of the biggest reasons that individual investors bought or sold. A user on a brokerage site might see the news breaking and get inspired to make trades, which was the way the brokerage sites made money. And as long as customers were seeing our news on the brokerage site, they wouldn't see the ads for the brokerage's competitors that were all over the Marketwatch.com site.

Because advertising revenue had dropped, we were under pressure, from both board members and outside analysts, to put all our information behind a pay wall, but we preferred to be diversified in our approach. We were making money both from ads and from licensing on the same content, and when advertising came back strong, we wanted to be in a position to benefit. With this flexible approach to pricing and revenue streams, we rode out the tech crash that wrecked so many businesses. In retrospect, it was great training for the C-scape: no single approach to revenue is likely to remain the best choice. Safety—and profits—lie in testing as many approaches as possible, using the ones that work, and keeping an eye out for the inevitable next wave of changes.

12

PARTNER LIKE A START-UP

ENTREPRENEURIAL ALLIANCES CURE
ORGANIZATIONAL OVERWHELM

It was 1991, and my partner, Ed Anderson, and I wanted to launch a new business. We wanted to serve sports fans with a handheld device that would give updates on all the games and sports news that mattered to them. This was before the Internet, before satellite television and satellite radio, even before fans could get scoring updates on their phones or their beepers. The "displaced fans" who lived or worked in one town but rooted for a team from another couldn't watch or listen to games; they could barely get out-of-town sports news after the game was over. ESPN sometimes provided scores, but it offered far fewer sports news programs than it does today. There were few sports talk radio stations then, and those that existed only covered local teams. Real fans would buy *USA Today* just to get one paragraph of information on their favorite pro or college teams.

We felt sure we had a strong concept, but we started out with only a few of the elements we needed to build the business. I brought a newspaper editor's understanding of what sports fans wanted and knowledge of the worlds of sports business and sports gaming. My partner brought the relationship with Data Broadcasting Corporation (DBC), the company that had created QuoteTrek, the subscription-based handheld device that delivered real-time stock quotes to brokers. We would use their technology and network for our product. We also had a small amount of money that we raised from friends and family. We knew we needed to preserve that money as long as possible if we had any chance of making the company a success. Everything else, we soon realized, we would have to get through partnerships.

We offered a little piece of our company to DBC, who agreed to convert a version of the QuoteTrek to a sports device and let us use their network, which was a radio signal on the FM Sideband, transmitted through dozens of radio stations around the country. The device, which we named Sportrax, looked something like the old "brick" cell phones, a narrow black rectangle with a stubby antenna and a small, square black-and-white screen that received text but no photos or video. It came with a pop-on stand so it could sit on your desk and alert you as sports news came in. We planned to offer the device for rental at $49 a month.

But we had no staff and no office. We had limited money to hire a staff or pay to manufacture our devices. Meanwhile, DBC was facing a cash-flow crisis, as their parent company was in bankruptcy. As a result of that crisis, DBC couldn't give their engineers raises. We didn't have a lot of cash, but we had a little, so we partnered with them in another way. They agreed to give us a little office space, and to let their engineers moonlight with us. That gave their staff a new source of income, which kept them from leaving, and it gave us access to a variety of experienced engineers without having to offer them full-time employment. They also offered us advances against the hardware because they could mask those costs in their production budgets.

Now we had an office and a product, but we still needed marketing, which we couldn't afford either. Instead of taking the traditional approach, we found a stodgy but well-respected magazine, the *Sporting News*, which was owned by the Times-Mirror newspaper company. We offered them a swap: their name on the device plus a piece of the profits if they would promote the product in their pages. We renamed the product *"The Sporting News* Sportrax," and now we had a marketing plan with no marketing expense.

Finally, there was one kind of data we wanted to provide on Sportrax, because it was available nowhere else. That was gambling odds. There was a demand from heavy sports betters to get real-time indications of the changes in the odds at each major casino. If a bettor knew the line on a game was changing, and knew it before the bookie he bet with, it could help in knowing when to put a bet down, and make a difference between winning and losing. The casinos, meanwhile, needed to know what the heavy bettors were doing, so they couldn't get outmaneuvered through a betting ploy known as "middling." We offered that if they would give us their own data, we would share the data from all the other casinos in real time, an arrangement that would protect them from middling. When the casinos agreed, we had sports odds data that no one else had—and we had a viable business.

Launching Datasport taught me how partnerships could rescue a business that is facing overwhelming demands—and in the C-scape, the number of different challenges and opportunities keeps increasing: new approaches to product design, new approaches to distribution, new platforms for marketing, new marketing methods, and new options for pricing and revenue streams. Add to that list consumers, clients, and colleagues who can't be controlled, but must be listened to and considered and answered in ongoing, unpredictable, convergent relationships. *Who can do all this?* Who has the time, the money, the resources, the creativity, and the patience?

Like Saul Bellow, who found that trying to digest the entire *New York Times* each morning gave him writer's block; and like the *New York Times* itself, which found, several years later, that it couldn't possibly report "all the news that's fit to print" on its own anymore (and started linking to other news providers on its website), any business that pays attention will see more changes and more new opportunities than it can handle alone. The C-scape brings a constant threat of organizational overwhelm.

But just as the cure for information overwhelm is curated help, the way to prevent drowning in the options and obligations of the C-scape is to seek help in the form of partnerships. As Bradley Inman, chief executive of digital e-book maker Vook, advised, "Partner like crazy."

Why should others partner with you when they are feeling the pressure as much as you are? Why should they work for your agenda when they have an agenda of their own? These are familiar questions, straight out of Management 101, at least when it comes to a manager supervising employees. And the answer has always been: in order to get what you need, you must think what others need and help them get it. What's new in the C-scape, as so many different aspects of business converge, is that this approach applies to more than just employees. It holds for customers, clients, suppliers, and business partners. They are all potential "consumers" of the "content" you offer, as I found when I launched Datasport. Entrepreneurial partnership explains why, at a time when so many established organizations feel overwhelmed with the sheer number of changes and possible responses, a new generation of entrepreneurs is not drowning, it's thriving.

One of these is Sarah Austin, a writer and video blogger who has built a business covering and advising the tech industry, and becoming in the process a kind of one-woman media conglomerate, an expert on social media and "micro-celebrity" who works with businesses ranging from Ford to T-Mobile and from Media Temple to Watchitoo.

She has created unique content, marketed it herself, and monetized it through corporate sponsorships. When Ford was looking to market a European model, the Ford Fiesta, to a young, web-savvy audience in the United States, they selected Austin as one of a hundred "Ford Fiesta Movement agents." Each one was given a Fiesta for six months to promote by using social media. After six months, according to Ford, the campaign, which involved no traditional media spending, inspired 4.3 million YouTube views, 500,000 Flickr views, 3 million Twitter impressions, and 50,000 interested potential customers, 97 percent of whom did not own a Ford. "Ninety percent of their target demographic—college students—are aware of the car," Austin explained. "I had a hard time parking anywhere on the UC Berkeley campus because crowds of students would surround my car to take pictures and ask for test drives."

Austin is paid for reviews on her blog and for consulting relationships with a range of companies. She has been featured on the cover of *Personal Branding* magazine and named by *Vanity Fair* as one of "America's Tweethearts," women achieving a new form of celebrity through social media such as Twitter. Her success is such that it seems to threaten her image as an ordinary blogger.

How did Austin turn herself, in her early twenties, into a hybrid tech and media company and an internationally known brand? From early on, in everything she did, she formed partnerships to achieve multiple goals: to understand the tech world, to publicize the activities and accomplishments of others in that world, and to build her own brand.

As a freshman in high school, she found a teacher to mentor her and encourage her early efforts with video. Lacking equipment, and hoping to produce quality web broadcasts that met high journalistic standards, she found people who had the equipment she needed and offered to work for them in exchange for loans. She began going to tech parties and tech events in northern California, bringing a microphone and a camera to interview people in the business, both unknown and highly influential.

From the start, she focused on creating content that would build word of mouth both for her interview subjects and for herself: "It wasn't just, 'I'll go interview somebody who's famous,'" Austin explained. "It was like, 'Do it in a certain way that no one's ever done before, that everyone has to go tell their friends about.'" Her approach to creating this unique content combined intelligence, irreverence, and her all-American newscaster good looks—on her website, you can find serious insights about marketing through social media, goofy stunts such as video of Austin wearing a Transformers costume to a drive-through restaurant, and glamour shots of Austin in the style of Hollywood actresses.

One day, while looking for a wireless signal in the park in San Francisco with a colleague who was lending her his laptop, she met John Draper, the famous phone hacker and compatriot of Bill Gates and Steve Wozniak, who was also struggling to get a wireless signal. Draper had appeared that day on the front page of the *Wall Street Journal*. The friend suggested that Sarah interview him, and that interview brought her to the attention of Gizmodo, the technology blog, which then sponsored her to cover tech events for them. Capitalizing on such serendipity has been the pattern for

Austin. Canny partnerships lead to opportunities to create media that benefit both her subject and herself, which lead to new partnerships. At the end of my interview with her for this book, she asked me to mentor her. Then she posted to her blog, "I'd like to proudly announce my new mentor," praising my work and linking to my biography. In the space of an hour or so we had become partners in three different ways—as writer and research subject, as mentor and mentee, and as online co-promoters of each other's professional efforts.

EVERYONE CONNECTED TO YOUR BUSINESS IS YOUR "CONSUMER"

Austin seems to treat everyone she meets as a consumer in the market for her compelling content. It's an approach at the heart of many successes in the C-scape, both small scale and large. Jacques-Antoine Granjon of Vente-privee (and inspiration for American discount-sales sites such as Gilt, Rue La La, Ideeli, and others) built his entire business by treating not just the customers who bought from him but also the suppliers who provided his merchandise as his consumers. He offered them all the same thoughtful service. "My job is to sell the collection of the people who worked hard to make them," he told me, stressing his obligation to serve their need. "I go to Abercrombie or Ralph Lauren, and I say: What service can I do for you? What inventory is left? I'll give you the best service. I'll take all [the excess inventory] you've got, and . . . sell a high volume at cost price, so you don't lose money." Granjon has succeeded in the C-scape because his attitude toward his suppliers was the same as his attitude toward his customers. They need something, and he can provide it.

In a similar way, the revenue-sharing approach that Condé Nast's

David Carey described in the last chapter was based on providing valuable content, not just to the magazine's readers but to its sponsors. What do companies that buy advertising want? They want buyers for their products, of course. Carey offers to provide those buyers, not just by selling space for advertising but in a long list of ways. "What business are we in?" Carey asked, framing the essential question for the magazine conglomerate. "We are in the community-building business. We aggregate communities around common interests and we create a lot of passion, in print, online, at events and in social media. That's our core competency. We can find people who love design or travel or whatever and create this network effect in every format available." And if Condé Nast can provide access to consumers who are fired up about the experiences their sponsors offer, and turn them out in every possible way, it has the basis for a larger partnership with businesses of all kinds, one that goes far beyond the traditional relationship of media outlet and sponsor.

Condé Nast has begun to offer companies that advertise with it data about the digital habits of their readers to use in their marketing efforts. Say a luxury brand wants to target Condé Nast readers who have purchased first-class airline tickets online, visited a Four Seasons hotel, and visited a Lamborghini showroom. The magazine can help them target their online advertisements to those readers. It can also help organize themed events that gather those readers in one place. "We need to be in the data business," said Carey. "We need to be in the events business. Our clients are going to market in every segment, and there's no reason we can't participate in every segment, other than just media. . . . So before you put in a flagship store, why couldn't *Vogue* provide some retail data and maybe overlay trend information on top of it?" This new opportunity represents a reinvention of the magazine company, like the reinvention of Hasbro we saw in Chapter 9, but this change comes from the other direction: Hasbro started in toys and games and moved into media; Condé Nast started in traditional media and committed to partnering in non-media areas such as travel, design, and sports. The point for Condé Nast is to make itself a compelling business partner for these companies in all their marketing efforts, not just a place to buy advertising. Every company must reinvent itself to combine media and business elements, and it will take partnership to do it, whether it is partnerships between individuals and companies or partnerships within single organizations.

The first step is to recognize the different "consumers" a business needs to serve and to make employees aware that the company has multiple obligations. "We have three customers," Jason Kilar of Hulu, the online video service created through an unprecedented partnership among television studios, told Charlie Rose. "We have users, we have advertisers, and we have content partners. . . . And I'm not saying it's easy, but we constantly live that delicate balance between our three customers and not sacrificing one out of the three or two out of the three. That's a huge part of our culture."

Even at the organizational level, taking care of someone else's needs is as much a matter of culture and psychology as it is of practical assistance. As the CEO of MarketWatch, I would ask my staff whether something they were suggesting was good for our customers or our partners and not just good for us. Ultimately, that question became part of how we made decisions. Sometimes it seemed we thought more about the interests of our partners or customers than they did, but that was part of providing what would "delight" them as often as possible. Once, we wanted to hire two full-time TV anchors to provide web video updates and work on a still-unsold idea for a weekly television show. We couldn't justify hiring two people for these tasks, but I suspected that if the new anchors were also available to CBS for urgent TV news reporting, the new hires would be worth the expense. No one had asked us to do this, but when we found two news anchors we liked, we asked CBS to interview them for us, and to evaluate them on the standard of what they would put on the air. When we hired the two new anchors, we put them in our office in CBS News in New York, and it only took a few weeks before CBS asked to "borrow" one for a complicated high-profile story. Soon they were appearing regularly on CBS stations, and each time Market-Watch received branding and credit on the air.

PARTNER APPEAL

I've referred to the famous story about the railroad industry not re-alizing that it was in the transportation business, rather than the railroad business, and I've suggested that all businesses must re-consider their core competency. But asking what business you're in is not enough. Success in the C-scape requires partnerships; part-nerships require treating multiple constituencies as if they were key consumers; so the question must become, "What business*es* are we in?" And to succeed in multiple businesses at once, it's necessary to be an appealing partner for all of your constituents. Kilar of Hulu says, "Our rallying cry as a company is to make sure that we de-liver a service that users, advertisers and content owners unabash-edly love, which means that the design of the service has to delight advertisers as much as it delights users, and we're not willing to settle for less than love, to be quite frank."

What are the approaches that make for "love" and "delight" among business partners?

DO ONE THING WELL.

Bradley Inman of Vook told me, "The idea of master media companies controlling distribution, content, and advertising platforms is over. Companies need to pick one thing and do it well. Take Craigslist or Google. Both are media companies, but they do *one* thing well—advertising." Google of course has many activities and ventures, but what made them an essential partner for so many other businesses was their ability to pair buyers and sellers according to interests revealed through Internet searches. That was the distinctive "content" they offered, and it drew companies into alliances that made their success as a partner possible.

SUPPORT PARTNERS FOR THE LONG TERM.

In the C-scape, no one knows all the changes coming tomorrow, or when a thriving organization will find itself struggling. When things are going well for a company and perhaps not so well for its partner, that is the best time to offer to help. Just as the C-scape rewards those companies that can develop long-term convergent relationships with customers, it does the same for long-term business partners.

SPREAD YOUR RISK.

In the C-scape, companies and individuals need to engage in multiple business ventures with multiple partners to create multiple revenue streams. Not all of these ventures will succeed, and even the successes are unlikely to come right away or consistently. Like venture capitalists, almost everyone in business will benefit from placing many small bets. When we founded Datasport, we thought that our market was "displaced sports fans," and that gamblers following the odds data would be secondary. As it turned out, most of the sports fans returned the Sportrax receivers after their free introductory month expired, saying they loved the product but the subscription price was too high. It was the gamblers who kept us in business by ordering even more, because having access to real-time odds made them money. That second constituency turned out to be the most important one for us. Even so, there weren't enough gamblers to make Sportrax a mass-market hit. In the end, over five years, we were able to create a successful business-to-business product for the sports gaming industry. DataSport brought its investors a healthy return, and it taught me several lessons that were significant in developing what would become MarketWatch. But we couldn't have pulled it off if we hadn't built it to appeal to three different constituencies—sports fans, gamblers, and the gaming industry—in a sense, three different business ventures in one.

CONVERGENT ENTREPRENEURSHIP

Successful partnership of the kind I'm describing means blending traditional corporate approaches with entrepreneurship, not just to establish start-ups but even after businesses are established and thriving. Acting in an entrepreneurial way, however, can be challenging in the traditional corporate world. Entrepreneurism is for people with a high risk profile, people willing to take bigger chances for a bigger success. That's the opposite risk profile of most people who succeed in large corporations, who often seek work in large, established companies because they want the benefits of success with as little risk as possible.

Most of the successes I've seen, including our own at CBS MarketWatch, have come from isolating entrepreneurial divisions from most regular practices of the parent company. Even though we were partly owned by CBS, they didn't interfere with the day-to-day running of the company. They didn't hire or fire our employees and they didn't hold us to their ways of doing things internally. In that way we could go on doing what we did well, creating a convergent financial news site, but with the advantage of the CBS brand. Our reporters and ad sales people had their calls returned because, to the outside world, they were part of CBS. And they behaved as if they were, respecting the CBS brand and working hard to please CBS every time we could, but preserving our independence.

We gave them use of our talent to help them stay competitive in business news on both TV and radio, and in the end, we convinced CBS that putting our brand name up on the CBS network was helpful to the network as well as to us. At that point we said that we had built our brand and it was as important to them as theirs was to us. This was a significant change, because from that point on we didn't want to "pay" for them to put our brand on TV. It was just part of the relationship in which two companies were giving each other something of value, and we could point to all the things we were doing for them (even though they hadn't asked for a lot of them, they were using them). Based on that two-way relationship, which we built by being overly generous with our time and resources, CBS agreed to keep promoting us and not charging us for the privilege.

Success in the C-scape depends on achieving true convergences of established brands and start-up culture, which often means nurturing a higher-risk style, one that will make possible big successes while tolerating some failures along the way, within the low-risk culture of most large corporations. In my experience, it takes changes of two overlapping kinds. Some are financial changes in business practices, but others, just as necessary, are changes—or at least work-arounds—for the existing corporate culture.

Today, when I advise a company preparing to acquire a start-up or launch a new division to address some aspect of the C-scape, I recommend these changes based in part on the MarketWatch experience.

KEEP THE PEOPLE YOU BRING IN.

So often I've seen companies make smart hires or strategic acquisitions, then become uncomfortable when management realizes that the new people in the company don't do business in the company's traditional ways. So they let the new people go, or the system purges them. People in traditional companies are often much better at knowing why something can't be done than how it can be done, and management often seems to forget that most of what made the hires or the acquisition so appealing was that they offered something new. Success comes from letting the people that seemed so successful outside of the company *do the same things within the company* that attracted attention in the first place.

When Hasbro began its partnerships with film, television, and video game designers, it shifted to a pay-for-performance model for most of its employees. Pay was now based on a combination of performance of the corporation as a whole, performance of the specific brands the employee worked on, in all formats (television, movies, traditional sales, licensing, and so forth), and on measures of individual performance. In this way, the new strategic goals of the entire company, which had been the reason for its new media partnerships, also became the basis for individual performance reviews and compensation.

REWARD RISK-TAKING.

Make sure the staff is motivated to take chances and gets rewarded for doing so. This approach means recognizing efforts within the management team even if they don't succeed. It also means giving people who take chances and fail even bigger assignments. When it comes to compensation, it means taking a long-term view and not punishing short-term setbacks. Often it's necessary to minimize Human Resources' role in hiring and performance reviews because traditional HR tends to categorize and limit employees in order to "pay within range," and makes it hard to reward extraordinary performers with appropriate bonuses.

ENCOURAGE OPTIMISM.

Believe that no matter how many times a potential deal dies, it can be resurrected. Individuals, divisions, and entire companies all have to maintain confidence despite huge odds, so that optimism can fuel the persistence and inventiveness that will prove it correct. While blind optimism can be deleterious, employees need to spend as much time as possible seeking ways to make a concept succeed.

BACK UP RISK-TAKING WITH FISCAL PRUDENCE

As a cultural style, risk-taking might seem like a natural match with carefree spending, but what's needed is actually the opposite. What risk-takers need most is the chance to try, and try again, and that is only possible when resources have been allocated to fund follow-up attempts. That's why, even as I recommend protecting the entrepreneurial culture, I also insist on conservative spending. Here are some changes in financial practices essential to success.

HOLD EXTRA CASH.

So many unanticipated events in the C-scape require extra cash. Product development can be delayed by illness of a staffer or contractor. Marketing costs can soar based on market conditions that

are out of control. Opportunities may come along to achieve substantial discounts in costs if it's possible to buy in bulk. In addition, running short on cash makes a company appear desperate;
getting more cash will cost a much larger chunk of the company as
the source of that cash sees the opportunity to squeeze more own-
ership out of you.

AVOID "VALUE TRAPS."

Don't pay for anything you can get just as well through barter,
earned media, or partnerships with other businesses. Every business has many untapped sources of value for its partners, and may
well need them all to run as if it were multiple businesses. David
Jackson, founder of the financial information site Seeking Alpha,
has built a world-class company around this principle. His site
provides investors with stock recommendations from some of the
most successful and insightful portfolio managers in the world,
but Jackson doesn't pay any of them. They post their predictions
and stock-picking advice to his site in return for the exposure
it gets them—many investors who read the site are looking for
money managers, whom they often choose based on what those
managers post.

As Jackson explains, paying even a small amount for stock recommendations is, for him, a "value trap," like a stock that, although
it has fallen in value, is still fundamentally overpriced. He will still
pay journalists for certain kinds of financial *news* that he can't get
otherwise, but the heart of his business is the trade he makes with
the money managers who write for him. He acts as curator, selecting only the best financial advisors to appear on Seeking Alpha,
and in exchange for his seal of approval and the exposure the site
offers, they provide their unique content: stock recommendations.
It's a great example of curation as a partnership strategy.

KEEP OVERHEAD LOW.

Not just spending on content, but spending of any kind should be avoided if it doesn't directly build the customer experience and the customer relationship to the brand. In particular, avoid expensive marketing or PR efforts that don't result in an improved product or product experience. Don't necessarily pay for highly automated systems that allow you to hire fewer customer service reps, unless they improve the customer experience. This was the mistake made by Webvan, the grocery delivery service that ordered a billion dollars worth of high-tech warehouses from the engineering company Bechtel in an effort to guarantee delivery of groceries to customers within a thirty-minute window. Their spending on infrastructure bankrupted them. It's better to put money into the quality of the product and into direct contact with consumers.

SELL OFF LEGACY ASSETS.

In the C-scape, just as products only have value to the degree that they are part of an experience that the consumer values, a company's assets, from its equipment to its real estate, only has value based on its contribution to the ongoing consumer experience. This idea can come as a shock to those impressed by a business's traditional trophy assets. The *San Francisco Chronicle*, for example, sold its printing presses and real estate and contracted with an outside printer to print the newspaper. A printing press had always been considered essential to a newspaper, but in the Internet age the huge costs of printing and delivering a newspaper no longer do anything to improve the content a news organization delivers to its customers. Instead, by cutting production costs, news organizations can cut the eventual costs to consumers for their news. It was wise to make printing a variable cost that could be adjusted downward as the market continued to change.

In a sense, this is the ultimate content strategy, expanding Jeff Jarvis's marketing rule, "do what you do best and link to the rest," to every aspect of business.

MEASURE COMPANY SUCCESS BY PROFIT, NOT TOP-LINE EARNINGS.

It's traditional to measure the success of a company according to its gross earnings. Often that's the first piece of data that business people, and particularly investors, want to know. Yet as digital media increasingly offers the ability to track the impact of spending, what we'll find most of the time is that top-line spending will decline. It's increasingly possible to know about company spending in general what John Wanamaker famously wished he knew about his spending on advertising—which half is wasted. Yet it is hard for managers and shareholders to understand that if a traditional company shrinks by half but keeps its profits steady, that might be the greatest win the C-scape can offer.

The emphasis on profit is especially important in the early years of a start-up. In fact, one of the recurring themes across companies I've profiled in this book, from Facebook to MarketWatch to Nespresso to Vente-privee and many in between, was an early, dual focus on profitability and the consumer experience, a focus that helped those companies stay out of bankruptcy long enough to get their business models right.

BRIDGING THE GAP BETWEEN TRADITIONAL AND NEW CULTURES

I advise companies all the time to separate their entrepreneurial divisions from the larger corporate culture and to follow the principles I've just laid out. But the world is messy, and it's not always possible to keep two business cultures separate. I've seen many failures of corporate-cultural convergence, some spectacular, like the AOL/Time Warner debacle I described at the start of this book, many less well known but equally avoidable. That's why, since I left newspaper journalism, I have spent much of my career as a translator, going back and forth between traditional and new-media businesses, helping them learn to partner for the benefit of both.

When I started a Digital Media division for CBS, serving as its first president, we had the rights to put March Madness college basketball playoffs online, but although everyone agreed that the playoff tournament was valuable content, no one at CBS had done much with those rights. Their website allowed users to pay to see any game they wanted online, but management was nervous about their ability to deliver quality live video on the web, so they never promoted it. When I arrived, they had tried to sell access to the games online, but only about 25,000 people had ever used it, while the television audience ranged from 6 to 10 million per regular season game, and more for the finals.

I believed that if we could offer the games for free online, supported by advertising, we would attract huge numbers of viewers, because the NCAA Tournament was the single best kind of live content possible for the Internet. Why? Most college basketball fans are loyal to their school teams but move away from their college towns after they graduate. Not only are the fans dispersed, but the playoff games themselves are dispersed across the country with no logic. A northeast team might play a southern team on a court out west. All you could be sure of, if you were a fan, was that the game available to you on local TV was probably the wrong one. But on the web, we could build a grid where each fan could see the game he or she wanted to see, giving consumers what they wanted, wherever they were, and giving advertisers a chance to sponsor a game whose audience was passionate and devoted.

The sticking point, as it is so often, was conflicting approaches to the brand among the people who had to partner for the venture to succeed—in this case, those with traditional backgrounds and those from a more entrepreneurial web background. The television people had worked for years to provide a reliable, high-quality television experience for their viewers, which was, and still is, better-looking and more consistent than any online video. They had steady income from advertisers, and they were afraid that expanding to online programming would decrease their on-air ratings and scare off advertisers who didn't want to support "iffy" production quality.

The web people, though, were used to taking a beta approach, trying out several alternatives and letting users tell them what worked. That only scared the TV people more. All they saw was the potential downside: We would embarrass ourselves because the video quality would be poor. Or, too many viewers would log on and we would "break the Internet." Or, too few would log on and we'd be embarrassed by the poor showing, thus alarming advertisers. Worst case, ratings would be so low that we would have to give back money or precious TV air time to those advertisers who bought spots on the web.

The TV people saw everything that could damage the brand and that was all they saw—they couldn't imagine how moving to a new platform could enhance the brand and the long-standing relationship between CBS and its viewers. These were all smart and successful TV programmers, the best in the business, but at the time, many of them would have preferred not to put TV programming on the Internet at all.

Often I doubted if the two groups—traditional media managers and the new-media teams—could work together. It took time and patience to show the web people that the TV people had a lot to lose, in terms of both reputation and revenue, and that they needed to have their concerns addressed with practical solutions. At the same time, I had to make clear to the TV people what the web people could see: that this tournament was the ideal event to put on the Internet. I worked to explain the concerns of the TV people to the tech people, so they could build software that would ease their fears.

Now, when fans logged on, the site didn't take them straight to a game. They had to start in a virtual "waiting room," which allowed us to control access and make sure there was always enough bandwidth to provide a quality picture. On the web side, we hadn't focused on that issue early on. We believed that if users couldn't get a good signal, they would understand, chalk it up to Internet problems, and come back later. But that wasn't good enough for a network. We had to show the TV executives that under no circumstances would we crash. On the other side, we had to convince the TV people that web access to the games wouldn't hurt traditional viewing on TV, where they made most of their money. We convinced them by arguing that what their consumers wanted, most of all, was to see the teams they loved, and second, to see as high quality a picture as possible. If "their" game was on both TV and the web, they would prefer TV. If "their" game was not on TV, or if viewers only had access to a computer (say, at work) the web was a terrific alternative. Huge numbers of fans who would have tuned out or just not been able to watch instead put up with the "lesser" experience of a web picture to see a game that mattered, creating an enormous new audience.

In all these ways, the web people went out of their way to protect the TV brand, far more than any Internet company would have done on its own, and CBS agreed to put the games online as we proposed. It was an eye-opening step for CBS and for the division: starting the first year with 1.5 viewers and $4 million in revenue. By 2008, it had over 4 million; in 2009, over 7 million, with no end to the growth in sight. By 2010, CBS estimated $40 million in revenue for the web games alone.

Such cultural standoffs between the traditional and the new have now become common across consumer-facing businesses. The only solution is to work for similar convergences of differing corporate cultures. To achieve such convergences, traditional brick-and-mortar brands such as Macy's and Bloomingdale's have worked to create partnerships between their online and traditional operations. The success of direct-to-consumer sales for macys.com and bloomingdales.com (over $1 billion in 2009) led the companies, which are jointly owned, to a greater focus on online marketing. They realized that another $5 billion or more in store sales were influenced by the Internet: when customers saw something they liked online, they later came into a store to buy it. "We have long since stopped looking at stores and online as separate silos," explained Terry J. Lundgren, chairman, president, and CEO of Macy's, using the language of web design—"silos"—to describe real-life sales.

Macy's management recognized that such influence could go both ways: if a customer saw something he or she liked in the store, but in the wrong size or color, then the store itself could become a media asset, driving later online sales. However, there were obstacles. There was delay and inconvenience for the customer who had to wait, get to a computer, remember the product, make time in a different part of the day to order it, and so on. That led management to the idea of "Search & Send," a system operated by sales associates at each in-store cash register, by which they can place an online order for delivery to the customer's home. To make Search & Send successful, though, management had to break down the old cultural divide between the store and the website, not just in their own minds but in the minds of their employees. Sales associates did not think of themselves as *partners* with online retailers. If anything, they saw the website as competition—the same cultural conflict we faced at CBS with March Madness online. For that reason, Lundgren says that management is "constantly communicating with our associates about the benefits of multichannel retailing so that they understand that our best customers shop us both in-store and online."

The key to partnerships both between companies and within them is to teach those who are part of both the traditional and the new-tech cultures to recognize that this isn't about the right way and the wrong way, but rather two different ways to add value, both necessary, with benefits for all. The entrepreneurial group must understand how the mainstream business has built and protected the value of the existing brand. Similarly, the traditional parts of the company must be motivated to take more risks in listening and responding to the changing needs and preferences of its customers. The key shift comes when the panicked and overwhelmed psychology of "How do we save our brand or business?" turns to a willingness to try a bunch of new approaches, even though only some will succeed—the beta approach, retooled for a convergent world.

13

THE NEW NEWSROOM

WHY EVERY BUSINESS NEEDS ONE

What makes the difference between success and failure in the C-scape? Here's a traveler's snapshot of both, as seen from a seat on an airplane.

First, failure. I recently boarded a Delta flight that was delayed for technical reasons. We boarded the plane, but then it sat on the runway. You might think that would have ruined my experience, but I was thrilled—not because the flight would be late, but because the airline had switched on their live television system and there was a college basketball game that I wanted to see. I turned on the game, but a few minutes later a flight attendant came over the public address system and started to make a series of announcements. She spoke slowly, drawing out her remarks. Her intention was no doubt considerate: an old-media attempt to fill the time while we waited by "broadcasting" some distracting chat, like an emcee telling jokes until the star of the show is ready to perform.

However, the flight attendant seemed not to realize that every time she spoke, a large visual box covered most of the screen of every TV on the plane and froze the action behind it. She left such long pauses as she spoke that the game would come on, and then freeze when she spoke again. This interruption happened again and again. Her traditional attempt at distracting us with the public address system was spoiling our chance to choose for ourselves from the new-media options the airline had provided, the televisions on the seatbacks. When she finished, halftime had begun. I felt frustrated—with her, with the delay, and with the airline overall. It would have been simple enough to pause the television entirely during the announcements, and then start it again once the flight attendant was done speaking, but either no one had thought to tell her or she had not received the message.

Afterward, I told the story repeatedly, venting my frustration to family and friends. I even put it in this book. That bad experience turned me into a one-man bad-publicity machine for that airline, because they had all the technology they needed to provide a great passenger experience even in poor circumstances, but they lacked the coordinated communication to follow through.

Now here's a success. A different flight on a different airline. According to Porter Gale, vice president of marketing for Virgin America, a passenger aboard a Virgin America flight, upset about not receiving a sandwich from the flight attendants, tweeted his frustration from midair using Virgin's Internet connectivity. Virgin has a big presence on social media sites, and one of its employees read the frustrated tweet, researched the hungry passenger's flight and seat number, and sent a message to the pilot. The pilot relayed it to the cabin crew, who brought the man a sandwich. Surprised and satisfied, he tweeted again, this time full of appreciation for the airline, revising his public negative brand message into a positive one before the plane even touched the ground.

Both airlines were making use of new-media technologies to try to improve the customer experience, but one coordinated that effort among its employees and the other did not. The difference between success and failure was coordinated, flexible communication.

TWO-WAY TALK

As we've seen, the C-scape has created tremendous pressure on almost every aspect of business, including product design, marketing, sales, customer relationships, revenue, company organization, and partnerships. Yet meeting these many challenges takes only one basic mechanism: two-way, responsive communication between organizations and their "consumers" of all kinds. To succeed, a company must:

1. Provide the news and information consumers need. Create the content and offer it directly, point consumers where they need to go to find it, or mix both broadcast and curation. Use every possible way to send your messages, from digital to telephonic to online and in-person. Treat each form as potentially the most important, since different constituents will prefer each one—and the same constituents will prefer different ones at different times.
2. Feed the underlying interests or concerns that shape the consumer experience. Create and curate not just news and practical information but entertainment, education, events, and partnerships. (This is what Delta was doing when it installed the capacity to show live TV on some of its flights.)
3. Host the larger conversations around the subject of the consumer experience, so that the talk about the organization happens where the company can listen and join in. (Join outside conversations that are relevant to the organization, too—this is

what Virgin was doing when it made a commitment to monitoring Twitter, a kind of internal curation of consumer feedback.)

4. Connect individually with consumers and develop long-term relationships that are of value to both sides, to tie consumers to the company for good.

That list doesn't sound much like traditional business communications. Nor does it sound like a traditional newsroom. What it does sound like is the convergent news-and-culture organizations that have become popular online, such as HuffPost or the Daily Beast. I think of this model as the "new newsroom," and it is an essential point of convergence between business and media. Every business must have a new newsroom in some form; every media company must become one; and success will depend on how well companies of all kinds integrate that "newsroom" with their traditional businesses.

On the Daily Beast, at the left side of the website you find links to traditional content (text and video) created by paid journalists hired and edited by the site in the traditional way. Down the center you find the Cheat Sheet ("Must reads from all over"), which is pure curation, a series of links to the content of all kinds that the Beast's editors think are most important that day. The third part, the Buzz Board, opens up the site to broader conversation, inviting guests to share their favorite new discoveries in many categories of interest to their readers. The site also encourages users to comment on all their stories, involving them in the storytelling process. Authors reply to those comments, so the story becomes customized according to readers' interests.

What keeps the site from becoming impossibly large is that founding editor Tina Brown uses her tastes and interests to define a community of people with similar interests and curates for the community that shares them. Her "subject" may not be as easy to define as NASCAR or the stock market, but it is a bundle of topics that interest her specific audience.

THE ROLE OF THE NEW NEWSROOM

For some organizations, depending on the consumer experiences they are working to create, the new newsroom may become the method by which they do most of their business. For Granjon of Vente-privee, success in the C-scape required a radical shift in technologies and methods. As the former clothing wholesaler put it, "I became a media person." His income derives entirely from online media interactions with his customers—they receive the company's emails, shop through the company's marketing media, and make their purchases online. Vente-privee is a superstore that is almost nothing but media.

By contrast, Johnson & Johnson has retained a far more traditional overall business model, yet the "new newsroom" they have created is just as sophisticated and diverse. Marc Monseau, the company's director of media relations, is a former reporter for Bloomberg News, which suggests that Johnson & Johnson understands that even a pharmaceutical company is in the media business. Its website offers the option to learn about company products, policies, and community programs either through videos or through written articles, whichever the user chooses. Further multimedia content addresses specific segments of its audience, including "text4moms," a yearlong subscription to information for expectant and new mothers that arrives by SMS message. Its YouTube channel has over ninety patient-education features. Multiple Facebook pages are oriented to different experiences of company products and patient medical conditions.

None of this would matter, however, if its convergent news operation weren't based on close knowledge of its audience. Expectant mothers post their concerns on the BabyCenter website, for example, instead of on other social networking sites, because BabyCenter serves their specific needs. As Tina Sharkey, chairman and global president of BabyCenter, told eMarketer.com, "When [a woman] becomes a mom, all her media usage goes down except for the Internet. Her engagement in the Internet actually goes up, and her reason for using the Web changes. Now, she's focused on information gathering." Expectant and new mothers also use the site to seek out new friends because their existing friends and family aren't usually at the same life moment, and may lack the knowledge and emotional perspective that new mothers seek. "In a mom social network like BabyCenter or others, she can get some really good advice and practical tips from people who understand and have empathy for her. Some 71% of BabyCenter moms say there's info they would put on BabyCenter that they would never share on Facebook." Like the Daily Beast, Johnson & Johnson's Babycenter.com attracts its audience by curating news, information, and community in convenient forms.

A NEW NEWSROOM THAT EVOLVES WITH THE C-SCAPE

The greatest challenge of the new newsroom, however, is not to set it up but to keep it relevant amid changing technologies and consumer choices. When Harvard Business Publishing discovered that its customer base was changing—and likely to keep changing—the company set out to reorganize. Adi Ignatius, who had been deputy managing editor at *Time*, became editor in chief of the new company. As he explains, "How people learn, how they read, what they'll pay for—all of this is evolving rapidly with the proliferation of information sources and technologies." At the urging of the company's board of directors, on which I sit, Ignatius and his partner, Josh Macht, editor and general manager of Time.com, spent the better part of 2009 drafting the blueprint for a new HBP, one better prepared to navigate the C-scape.

Previously, the company was made up of three separate entities: corporate and individual management training, book publishing, and magazine publishing. Now they decided to "smash the silos" of the three divisions of the company and roll them up into one. "We realized we weren't in the book and magazine business," said Macht. "We were in the idea business."

That means that each relationship with a potential author must start with a question: what are the best forms for presenting and marketing this author's ideas? Some will still start out as books, but others might be better tested as magazine pieces, online chats, even "tweet-ups," in which an audience for a live presentation and discussion is selected from the company's Twitter followers. Every platform, the company decided, has value, and though no one can define them all now, some of those new platforms were clear—the Internet and mobile platforms, among others. HBP wanted to be at the forefront of understanding how all platforms could play a role in spreading great ideas.

On these new platforms, authors could find not only a bigger readership but a more relevant readership, excited to interact with the author and to help the ideas evolve. An author might start with a magazine article, follow up with a blog, deliver a series of lectures, offer the lectures as podcasts, publish a book, and then follow up with educational software for managers, all under the auspices of HBP. Along the way, the company would be helping the author establish relationships with the kinds of businesspeople and business educators most likely to put his or her ideas into practice.

There are positive side effects of the reorganization for the company as well. Rather than having to commit to a book contract with every writer, the firm could start a relationship with a writer or teacher with a less ambitious effort, like an article or an online conversation. Then, if the author's ideas took hold, a book could follow. In these ways HBP is taking a convergent approach with benefits for all of its "consumers": its audience, its authors, and the company itself.

Similarly, when Nespresso first launched its line of espresso coffee, it faced two difficulties. First, its product, a sealed coffee capsule that only worked in machines designed to their specifications, was not well known. Second, the company had spent most of its money developing the product and had little left over for marketing. Unable to explain its new approach with traditional marketing, it decided instead to cultivate a direct relationship with customers. Retailers who sold its espresso machines explained to buyers that they would have to call Nespresso's Club for Connoisseurs to order their coffee capsules. As Arnaud Deschamps, head of Nespresso France, describes, "When they called, we had the opportunity to explain to them what we wanted to achieve: where we buy the coffee, the quality you find in the coffee, and so on. It was a fantastic chance to create a real relationship."

Initially, representatives at the call center worked from scripts, but many callers had interests and concerns not anticipated by the written scripts. So the call center employees were directed to ask customers whether they *wanted* to hear a standard explanation (the script) or whether they preferred to ask their own questions. In this way, Nespresso created a kind of "coffee channel," a comprehensive media source.

But it was more than that, because it included two-way conversation that gave the company a chance to learn what would improve their experience. "Most important," says Deschamps, "is to watch at each point of contact and be able to recognize behavior that can be translated into an action." A customer who called to say he or she loved the coffee would be contacted with opportunities for tastings and ongoing education about coffee. A customer who expressed relief that a shipment would arrive soon would be told about coffee subscriptions. A customer who returned empty coffee capsules to a store for recycling would be contacted later by a representative offering an environmental message—for example, news of an improved espresso machine that emits less carbon dioxide. From these conversations, the company identified categories of customer relationships they could develop, not according to standard demographic categories or the assumptions of marketers, but according to the interests that customers described: they categorized themselves as a "green" customer, a "coffee expert," and so on. In this way the company learned to refine the "news" it offered to keep it relevant to segments of its audience.

As the company grew, adding "coffee boutiques," a television advertising campaign, and a website, sales shifted. In time, 60 percent of coffee sales were done through the Internet, a third in boutiques, and less than 10 percent through the call center. At that point, had Nespresso spoken to any conventional business consultant, that consultant would have said: this is a great opportunity—downsize your call centers and reap the cost savings of Internet sales. But Nespresso did not want to lose the close relationship it had built with its customers. And the company observed that while sales through the call centers were down, the total number of calls was up. Nespresso customers still wanted to talk about coffee and to deal with problems in person. The company decided to invest even more in the call centers, to spend more time on the phone with the passionate customers who were its most important ambassadors. Even the Internet, according to Deschamps, was not as effective for spreading news of what the company offered. For his customers, Deschamps had discovered, the call center was an even better social network than Facebook or Twitter because customers actually *talked* directly to Nespresso.

THE MULTIPLIER EFFECT

Deschamps attributes Nespresso's success not just to the coffee centers but to the interactions among all of its media, traditional, new, and unusual, which allowed it to create ongoing personal relationships with customers that were also very profitable. As of 2009, word of mouth accounted for one out of every two sales, and Nespresso had averaged 35 percent annual growth over the past eight years.

Advertising guru Jon Bond explains this multiplier effect this way: every company has a variety of media assets, but most traditional marketers can't even identify all of them, let alone link them up together. He gives the example of his work with the fast food restaurant Wendy's, whose assets at one time included:

- *Paid media*, in the form of national television campaigns, for which Wendy's spent approximately $300 million per year;
- *Owned media*, in the form of thousands of retail stores, which attracted 77 million unique visitors per year. ("At that time," Bond explains, "the company didn't recognize their stores as media, just as places to sell burgers. Yet imagine what they would have been willing to pay for advertising that reached the same number of established Wendy's customers.")
- *Earned media,* or what we might also call *co-created media*: assets including its website, with 3 million unique visitors per

year; a Facebook page; and a database of over a million Wendy's fans called "Wendy Mail," which sent customers occasional coupons and special offers.

These substantial assets were not connected in any way. The TV ads never drove customers anywhere except presumably to the store. The stores did little to engage or move consumers to do anything other than eat their food and leave. The earned media was neglected—there was a Facebook fan page, but it wasn't part of a larger marketing campaign. All Wendy's had was a collection of disassociated media assets that encouraged consumers to do what they don't do anymore: stay still.

Bond organized a test at twenty Wendy's stores to see what would happen if Wendy's started inviting customers to move around among the different media assets in exchange for appealing content. Every time a customer bought food, his bag also included a two-cent card asking him to go to the website and sign up for Wendy Mail. Customers were promised a substantial coupon as the first of ongoing benefits for signing up. In two weeks, enough people joined that the company could project that rolling out this simple program in all Wendy's stores would increase the fan list from just over a million to 6 million. And for each dollar spent on the test, the company saw an increase in sales of $1.22—an "astonishing" result, according to Bond.

Once again, this success story was not a simple shift from traditional marketing media to digital. While Bond's test campaign used the company's new website and Facebook fan page, it also relied on signs hung in stores and printed paper cards dropped in shopping bags, technologies already available a century or so earlier, when the first hamburger was served. Follow-up included further additions to Wendy's Facebook page but also traditional television ads that encouraged viewers to seek out that page, which would in turn generate free media via both Facebook interactions and old-fashioned conversations.

To take full advantage of a convergent newsroom linked to all of a company's media assets, it's necessary to make some major strategic changes. Until recently, one of the "rules" of business was to measure the real lifetime value of a customer and decide what it was worth to get and keep that customer—making sure, of course, that the customer generates more money than the company spends on him. But in the C-scape, that can be a mistake, causing companies to lose "marginal" or "unprofitable" customers forever, even ones who could have become profitable later on. In the world of the C-scape, companies need to build relationships with customers without knowing exactly what that customer is worth, betting that the ultimate value of that customer will grow.

THE NEW NEWSROOM BUILDS ENTIRE BUSINESSES

The convergent newsroom can improve and sometimes replace not just traditional marketing and sales, but other traditional functions of a company, and sometimes even entire departments. Glen T. Senk, CEO of Urban Outfitters, explains, "We hire our own customers. You'd have to be deaf, dumb and blind not to know what's going on when kids are walking around talking about Facebook, [using] their iPhones, shopping online, and checking Craigslist to get apartments." By hiring customers who are already comfortable with aspects of the C-scape, the company adapts to changing conditions "organically," says Senk.

One teenage blogger, Jane Aldridge, caught the eye of an Urban Outfitters employee with her website, Sea of Shoes, which featured well-produced pictures of Aldridge herself modeling shoes and clothes in places that she thought suited them. Combining a sophisticated fashion sensibility with details of her personal life—pictures of trips with family or friends, pages from her favorite Japanese manga comic books—Aldridge seemed so perfectly matched to Urban Outfitters' style that the employee who admired her site proposed that she design her own shoe line. It had never been done before, but management agreed. Their new newsroom had become a recruitment tool for product designers, thanks to the responsiveness of one employee.

Quirky, a consumer products design company, uses its "new newsroom" to crowdsource the work traditionally done by a development staff. For $99, anyone with an idea for a consumer product can post that idea to the company's website, announcing to the Quirky community that he or she has a concept but needs help to make it a reality. Then, as the website describes, "Thousands of people—industrial designers, engineers, graphic artists, and average Joes—add their two cents throughout the process," offering suggestions for both design and marketing. Quirky's judges choose a weekly winner, and their staff creates professional design specifications for that item, pre-sells it on the website to raise funds for its production, finds a manufacturer to produce it and then sells the product on its site, sharing the revenue with the creator and the "influencers" who contributed ideas. Products have included a curved spoon that hangs from the edge of coffee mug, an iPhone case with a built-in light that doubles as a camera flash, and many other small innovations for home and office, none of which would exist today had "news" of the inventor's inspiration not been broadcast through the company's online media.

Exit41 offers a virtual call center for restaurants and restaurant chains, providing an alternative to having busy waiters and hosts answer the phones. Exit41 diverts patron calls to trained operators who know the restaurant's menu, recognize repeat customers, and can offer suggestions based on past orders and the restaurant's specials and sales goals. They can also follow up with marketing calls, email, and incentive programs to build customer loyalty. The goal of the company is to create the kind of high-level, two-way, ongoing customer relationships service that most restaurants lack the trained staff to develop themselves. It's the new newsroom, outsourced.

Etsy, an international online marketplace for handmade and one-of-a-kind products, uses their "new newsroom" not just for marketing, but also to recruit, train, and coordinate their suppliers and sales force. The core of their business is their sellers, typically sole proprietors who make their own products by hand, ranging from clothes and furniture to bath and beauty aids, from toys to weddings decorations. The sellers post photographs, videos, and descriptions of their wares for sale on the Etsy site. The company does little traditional marketing, and anticipates doing even less. According to Jesse Hertzberg, vice president of business operations, in 2009 Etsy spent roughly $300,000 in paid advertising and had $180 million in gross marketplace sales; for 2010 they projected doubling gross sales but cutting spending on traditional advertising by more than half. Instead of traditional marketing, Etsy spreads the news of its sellers' offerings and its own programs through its website and blog and through social networks; its sellers market their products through personal blogs and social networks. A member of the marketing team pitches stories about successful artisans and their products to traditional and online media outlets. "We want to be tastemakers," says Hertzberg.

The company creates online articles and short documentary videos about their sellers. "We are storytellers," says Hertzberg. "We sell stories. Every product has one: how it was made, why it was made, the artist's story." They also select artisans to profile in columns such as "Quit Your Day Job," which describes sellers who successfully made their craft into a self-supporting business, and offers tips for others hoping to do the same. Sellers compete to be featured on the site by creating individual web pages that catch the eye with photos, video, and text. Originally, much of the curation was done by Etsy staff, but as Hertzberg explains, "We don't want to be the curators. We want to create a platform and service where shoppers and sellers can curate as they wish." Gathering data on how the website is used, Etsy translates the behavior of its shoppers and sellers—the number of times a seller's page is viewed, the number of viewers who signal enthusiasm for a product on that page with a "heart," the volume of sales—into votes for featured artisans in different categories. In this way, Etsy lets the community decide who merits more attention on the website and blog.

The most ambitious sellers join "street teams," roughly seven hundred groups whose members live in the same area or share a craft specialty, such as crochet or dichroic glass. Coordinated through the Etsy site and blog, the teams socialize together, share craft techniques and observations about market trends, and help support one another in the sometimes lonely and confusing life of the solo artisan. Participation in street teams, says Hertzberg, helps sellers take steps from being hobbyists to being professionals.

Spread mainly across North America and Europe, the 35,000 artisans in these teams are the online company's physical ambassadors, marketing themselves jointly at trade shows and craft fairs. Rather than each individual artist paying a booth fee, they often share booths and travel expenses. Etsy subsidizes them through a grants program that can pay for ads in local papers, transportation, or promotional items. "The teams are probably our biggest marketing organization," explained Matt Stinchcomb, Etsy's vice president of community.

> *The smartest thing [Etsy does] is to focus on giving tools to community members. They can be more effective than we ever could. If we have 10K to spend, we can take out a quarter-page ad in a magazine one time or we can give it to our users and not only extend the gesture that makes them like Etsy more, but also help enable a marketing force of many more people that can reach a much bigger audience.*

Like a retail version of a flash mob, street teams come together for short periods of time to sell their wares, always promoting Etsy's site as the place consumers can find their products when the live event ends. In a sense, by helping to curate news and information about its sellers, Etsy crowdsources a chain of temporary, artisanal department stores, including suppliers, marketers, and retail staff. It's an example of online curation and convergence creating an entire offline business operation.

THE ONLY CONSTANT IS CHANGE

No one knows when the disadvantages of any given form will start to outweigh the benefits in a company's convergent newsroom. With the current explosion of interest in social media, for example, it's easy to miss the point Taddy Hall posted to Advertising Age, what he called the Martha Stewart Rule: "Throw your own party; don't just cater someone else's! If you base your social campaigns in venues you don't control—such as Facebook or YouTube—you may get great 'attendance,' but data show it's hard to convert and retain these party-goers. If your goals are anything beyond building brand awareness, it's better to have a house of your own where friends can find you." Jed Alpert, founder of Mobile Commons, says, "When you rely on social networking sites, you are handing your relationships off to those services and broadcasting to the group instead of developing one-to-one intimacy. The conversation is endlessly interrupted, and the resulting data about your customers isn't available for your marketing department." His company's approach is to design mobile campaigns in which his clients host their own text-message-based discussions, rather than relying on third-party sites, allowing them not just to listen in but to cultivate relationships with each participant individually, over time. He believes that is the future of making commenters into customers.

What to do about the chronic unpredictability of communication within the C-scape? Be open-minded about the forms that your communications may take. The habits of content consumers are ever changing. Don't place bets based on anyone's specific advice, nor on what is succeeding right now. Pay attention instead to consumers' ongoing discussions and behavior. Think how shocked cell phone makers like Nokia and Ericsson must have been when they realized that the biggest threat to their market share was coming from Apple—a computer company with no previous phone experience. They were probably as shocked as Nikon had been a few years earlier, when Nokia put cameras in cell phones and overnight became the biggest camera maker in the world. Companies must design their "news" content for and with their audience, but most of all, they must watch and listen to see how that audience uses it. Companies curate, but consumers still choose.

How can a company encourage employees to pursue the benefits of the new newsroom? In part, the answer is to recognize that coordinated two-way communication is now one of the core "products" of any successful business, and to establish its importance and reward for it across the entire organization. Hasbro, for example, has assigned Global Brand Leaders to make sure its brands are properly rendered in every different medium where they appear, among both internal and external company partners. Similarly, customer communication and e-commerce can't be set off in separate silos of a business, but must be integrated with the entire company. It's not enough to install the televisions on your airplane; the whole flight crew has to know how they work, and how they may conflict with traditional practices and forms of communication on the plane.

But that's only part of the answer to my question: how do you get people to act this way? "I don't know that you can get anybody to behave a certain way," said Urban Outfitters' Senk. "I think you can hire certain people. As a company, we like to hire people who are curious, people who are outgoing, people who always challenging the status quo and looking for what's next."

Jon Raj, who helped found the Visa Business Network, agrees that success depends on curiosity and a willingness to experiment with new approaches—before it's clear those approaches will work. "I see with a lot of companies that those slow to embrace new things can't then just hire one smart person and become innovative. You have to take the steps. The companies that have been testing and learning are the ones that will make it succeed." In the C-scape, tomorrow is always uncertain; your best bet is to partner with those motivated to change as the business world around them changes, navigating according to the four C's and communicating together as they go—and to become one of those people yourself.

ACKNOWLEDGMENTS

I worked on this book for over two years, but I've been learning the lessons that led me to write it for many years. I've been fortunate to have worked for and with some of the most amazing people in the media and in management.

First, I have had amazing bosses. Each took a chance on me and each taught me valuable lessons: Hal Buell at the AP; Katharine Graham, Don Graham, Ben Bradlee, Howard Simons, Len Downie, and Ed Padilla at the Washington Post Company; Will Hearst III at the *San Francisco Examiner*; Alan Hirschfield and Allen Tessler at Data Broadcasting Corp.; and Leslie Moonves at CBS.

As a journalist, I had some amazing editors: Marshall Loeb at *Time* magazine, Jim Wood at the *San Francisco Examiner*, and Peter Silberman at the *Washington Post* all mentored me as a writer and reporter.

As a young editor, watching my boss Ben Bradlee run a newsroom was like watching a great conductor. You could barely tell what he did, much less how he got things to happen. It looked effortless. But it was a rare form of brilliance. I'm not sure a lot of folks knew exactly why they would charge up the hill for him, but they would—and never look back. I would be right there with them.

Over the past two years I interviewed hundreds of people for this book. While many are named and quoted in the book, as many are not cited directly. But all of them contributed with their insights.

Former Harvard Business School professor Jeffrey Rayport, who now works in both consulting and private equity, and who served on my board of directors at Marketwatch.com, was one of the first people to encourage me to write this book. He gave me a tremendous foundation for it with long discussions about what was happening to the media companies today.

Another board member and former president of CBS News, Andrew Heyward, also helped me focus on the issues tearing up the media. He and Jeffrey recognized early that every company would become a media company, and helped me understand why. Several members of that board became mentors of mine, and helped me grow as both a manager and a leader, particularly Christie Hefner and Bob Lessin. Two of the bankers who advised us, Jeff Sine and Navid Mahmoodzadegan, also gave me a critical education in the financial underpinning necessary for businesses to run well.

Longtime friend and former Washington Post Company president Alan Spoon has given me a lifelong and invaluable series of lessons about media companies. He also supported my work at Polaris Venture Partners, which gave me a new appreciation of entrepreneurism and the risks and rewards of venture capitalism.

After I left the noble profession of journalism for a life of managing journalists, I was fortunate enough to hire sensational editors. They continue to make me look smart, and remain friends and important advisors. Dave Callaway, editor of MarketWatch.com, has been a constant source of tremendous insights into which companies are doing things right and which ones are doing things wrong. Rem Reider, editor of the *American Journalism Review*, has been a tireless chronicler of the fight to save journalism.

At the Newhouse School at Syracuse University, where I teach, they try to understand the future of journalism and how to help lead the media to the promised land. Former dean David Rubin and present dean Lorraine Branham, and professor Stephen Masiclat have both given me greater understanding into the strategies they need to fight the good fight and help an industry to save itself.

I had help in my overseas reporting from David Horovitz, the editor of the *Jerusalem Post*. He taught me to understand the cultural and societal forces that gave rise to the tremendous era of entrepreneurism sweeping Israel today. Bob Rosenschein, the brilliant CEO of Answers.com and a longtime friend, introduced me to many of the Israeli entrepreneurs and investors I interviewed for the book. He and his wife, Diane, hosted my visit to Jerusalem and carted me around the country for most of my interviews, including a wonderfully rambling dinner with Israeli entrepreneur extraordinaire Jon Medved and a fantastic meeting with venture capitalist Yossi Vardi.

In France the amazing Marie Laure Fleming arranged the interviews I had with the executives of Nespresso, Vente-privee, Bourcheron, and Bon Marche. It was an eye-opening series of interviews that revealed that most of these companies would make the changes necessary to survive in the future.

Several media executives helped me appreciate the depths of the challenges their companies faced and the extent to which they were taking them on. Many early discussions I had with MarketWatch COO Kathy Yates, who later went on to become CEO of AllBusiness.com, were tremendously helpful.

Bruce Campbell, president of Digital Media and Corporate Development of Discovery Communications did a tremendous job outlining Discovery's efforts to use partnerships as a key element of facing a changing media environment.

At Condé Nast, Steve Newhouse and David Carey, who has since become president of Hearst Magazines, gave me great insights into the complicated issues media companies face in trying to integrate new entrepreneurial media businesses into their traditional companies. At CBS, that was a constant theme of many valuable early discussions I had with network chief Nancy Tellum and my CBS Digital senior vice president Jon Sobel. Editor Ed Nardosa and publisher Dan Lagani at *Womens Wear Daily* helped me frame the unique issues surrounding B-to-B businesses facing the same digital challenges. NBC Universal's Lisa Gersh helped me understand the value and dangers in Media mergers and acquisitions.

John Makinson, chairman of Penguin Publishing and another former MarketWatch board member, provided enormous insight into the world of publishing, including educational publishing.

At Harvard Business Publishing, CEO David Wan and board chairman Howard Stevenson have led several conversations with me and other members of their board about the need to reinvent their company. Those discussions, and the subsequent work by editor Adi Ignatius and publisher Josh Macht, were foundational to my thinking about content in the digital age.

The remarkable CEOs of the boards I serve on were particularly helpful in giving me glimpses into the complexity of managing media businesses during this difficult transition period. David Pecker at American Media and David Zaslav of Discovery Communications are both executives with amazing track records. Pecker has saved his company, while Zaslav, in recent years, has made Discovery a media powerhouse. Both have shown me how creative leadership has helped their media companies to take advantage of the changing digital landscape, not just fear it.

Other discussions that were particularly helpful included talks with Rupert Murdoch and Robert Thomson of News Corp. after their purchase of Dow Jones (and therefore, MarketWatch), Tina Brown of the Daily Beast, Laureen Ong of the Travel Channel, David Green of September Films, Fredy Bush of Xinhua Sports and Entertainment, Rafat Ali of Paid Content, Laurel Touby of MediaBistro, Elizabeth Demarse of CreditCards.com, Kevin Wassong and Todd Harrison of Minyanville, Ralph Terkowitz of ABS Capital Partners, Pam Horan of the Online Publishers Association, and her husband, Peter Horan, who has led several digital companies. All provided valuable insights into the difficulties of working in an industry in transition.

In San Francisco some of my colleagues from my early days as a writer and editor were particularly helpful in giving me a perspective on the world of journalism today. Writer Carol Pogash and radio news executives Bruce Koon and Raul Ramirez all debated the future of our business late into the night at a series of regular dinners that have been going on for more than thirty years

There are countless journalists, bloggers, and venture capitalists who have helped me focus on the issues behind this book through their own writings. The *New York Times*, the *Wall Street Journal*, the *Washington Post*, and the *Harvard Business Review* all remain tremendous sources of ideas and thought leadership in business. Websites Paidcontent.org and MediaBistro, friends and bloggers Bill Bishop, Mike Hirshland, and Merrill Brown, venture capitalist Alan Patricof, analyst Colin Gillis, and private equity expert Brad Patelli are tops among the hundreds of sources I've used.

And there was Pam Kruger, who first approached me with the

idea for doing a book after hearing me speak. Picking up the ball from Pam was her agent, Fredi Friedman, who became my agent and convinced me that I not only *could* write this book, but that I *had* to do it. Fredi and her assistant Chandler Smith nudged me to get on with it over and over again.

Thanks also to Jonathan Burnham, Gretchen Crary, Mark Ferguson, Hollis Heimbouch, Matt Inman, Angie Lee, Ben Loehnen, Kathy Schneider, and everyone else at HarperCollins who worked on the book's behalf. It was this team that a year ago convinced me to broaden the book well beyond media.

Finally, I can't thank my family enough. My mom and dad supported my obsession with journalism from that first snowy day in 1962 Hackensack, New Jersey, when I started my paper route. To this day my best advice comes from my dad, Abe, who at ninety-two still follows my every move via computer and iPad. And, of course, my wife Myla and our kids Erika and Matt. They have always been supportive despite the toll it took on our time together. They were terrific sounding boards, particularly when I was venturing nervously into the youthful world of digital media.

INDEX

ABC (American Broadcast Company), 29
AccelGolf, 130–32
Acela Express, 143–44
acknowledgment of mistakes, 97–99
AdAge, 172
Ad Selector, 88
advertising, 69–90
  as content, 86–88
  convergence with entertainment, 79, 80–84
  convergence with news and information, 79, 84–86
  end of market segmentation, 88–89
  market as a relationship, 89–90
  marketers fighting back, 73–75
  new barriers to, 75–76
  paying consumers for their attention, 79–80
  purchase funnel, 71–73
Ad Week, 94
Agent 16, 103
aggregators, 44, 45–46, 53–54
airplane tickets, 128–30
Aldridge, Jane, 218–19

All the President's Men (movie), 25
Alpert, Jed, 223
amateurs vs. experts, 47–51
amateur TV, 62–65
Amazon, 118–19
  Kindle, 19, 112
American Express, 173, 177
American Idol (TV show), 62
Amtrak, 143–44
Anderson, Chris, 33
Anderson Analytics, 51
Anderson Cooper 360 (TV show), 102
Andrews Sisters, 119
Answers.com, 47, 49, 69–70, 86
AOL (America Online), 12–14, 109–10, 201
apologies (apologizing for mistakes), 97–99
Apple, 158–62
  iMovie, 28
  iPad, 19, 159, 161
  iPhone, 98, 99, 112, 113, 159, 223
  iPod, 39, 159, 160
  iTunes, 31, 39, 159–61, 170
  Lala, 31

App Store (Apple), 161
Aston Martin, 84
Atlantic Records, 170
AT&T Park (San Francisco), 84
Austin, Sarah, 187–89
Ayers, Roy, 81

BabyCenter, 179, 212
Baby Registry, 179
Banana Republic, 176
banking, convergent PR in,
    104–6
Bay, Michael, 97
Bechtel, 199
Bedos, Jean-Christophe, 88,
    107–8, 111, 112, 113–14,
    176–77
Bee TV, 145–49, 150, 158,
    161–62
Bellow, Saul, 44, 46, 55, 186
Benny, Jack, 80
Berlin, Irving, 24
Big Charts, 180
Bing, 79, 81–82
bing-a-thon, 79, 81–82
blast faxes, 93
Blockbuster, 11
blogs (bloggers), 47–51, 93–96
blogspot, 95
Bloomberg News, 211
Bloomingdale's, 204
Bond, Jon, 106–7, 121, 150,
    216–18
Boucheron, 88, 107–8, 111,
    113–14, 144, 176–77
"brand belongs to the customer,"
    74–75
Brandweek.com, 82–83
Brown, Tina, 210–11

Burger King's "Subservient
    Chicken," 83–84, 104
Burman, Tony, 85

cable TV, 29
Canadian Club, 108
Candlestick Park (San Francisco),
    84
Carat, 78
cardiologists, and blood pressure
    readings, 142
Carey, David, 168, 171–73, 178,
    190–91
Catalog Choice, 76
CBS (Columbia Broadcast
    System), 6–8, 192, 194–95,
    201–4
CBS Digital Media, 6–8, 201–4
CBS MarketWatch, 180–81,
    191–92, 194–95
CD Walkman, 39
Center for Investigative Report-
    ing, 64
Center for Television and Popular
    Culture, 62–63
chat rooms, 47–51
"Chinese wall," 85–86
choice. *See* consumer choice
Circuit City, 154
Citi Credit Cards, 105–6
classified advertisements, 37–38,
    41
click-throughs, 50, 87
CNN (Cable News Network), 7,
    29
Coatney, Mark, 74
Coca-Cola, 141–42
co-creation, 144–45, 149–50
Collier, Charlie, 82–83

company organization, 209–11
concierge marketing, 117–20
concierge pricing, 171–77
concierge product design, 145–49
Condé Nast, 168, 171–73, 178,
189–91
Condé Nast Traveler, 178
conservative spending, 197–200
consumer choice (consumers), 10,
23–33, 87–88, 144–45
acknowledging mistakes, 97–99
convergence with producers,
62–65
loyalty retention. *See* loyalty
paying for content, 39–40
paying for their attention, 79–80
power shifts to, 25–30
providing useful information,
79, 84–86
TV changes for, 25–30
"contact aggregators," 53–54
content, 10, 35–42
advertising as, 86–88
Apple and, 160–61
convergence of advertising with
entertainment, 79, 80–84
convergence of advertising with
news, 79, 84–86
delivery of, 36–38
paying consumers for their
attention, 79–80
product as, 127–32
shifting thinking on, 38–42
content aggregators, 44, 45–46
convergence, 10, 14–15, 57–65
of advertising and entertainment, 79, 80–84
of advertising and news, 79,
84–86

of consumers and producers,
62–65
in storytelling technology,
57–62
convergent entrepreneurship,
194–97
encouraging optimism, 197
hiring people, 196–97
rewarding risk-taking, 196–97
convergent newsroom. *See* new
newsroom
convergent PR, 93–97
cough syrup, 155
Coursey, David, 99
Craigslist, 193
Crain's New York Business, 91–92
Crawford, Joan, 80
Crazy Eddie, 154
Crossborders, 120–21
crowdsourcing, 105, 147–50, 219,
222
C-scape, use of term, 11
curation, 10, 43–55, 95–96,
209–10
amateurs vs. experts, 47–51
Apple and, 160–61
managing information overload,
45–46
managing social overload, 52–55
product design and, 149–51
Cushing Academy, 24–25
customer choice. *See* consumer
choice
customer loyalty, 30–33, 153–63
customer service, 109–21
as department, not a mindset,
114–15
reasons for providing better,
110–12

customer service (*cont.*)
  recognizing needs before being asked, 115–17, 120–21
  remembering past preferences, 117–20
  social networking and, 115–17, 120–21

Daily Beast, 210–11
Data Broadcasting Corporation (DBC), 184
Datasport, 184–87, 193–94
David, Paul, 54
deadspin.com, 94
delivery of content, 36–38
Dell, 110
Delta Airlines, 207–8
"democratization of news," 95
Deschamps, Arnaud, 153, 214–16
dial-up subscribers, 12–13
Diapers.com, 179
digital mindreading, 117–20
direct mail, 76, 106
Discovery Kids Network, 138
Disney Store, 156–57, 162
Donchin, Andy, 78
Do Not Call Registry, 76
Draper, John, 188–89
Drexler, Millard "Micky," 156
DVRs (digital video recorders), 29–30, 73, 77–78, 141

earned media, 216–17
ease of use, and consumer choice, 31
eBay, 30
Economist, 159
Edelman, Richard, 91, 96
Editor and Publisher, 94

Eidia Lush, 144
80-20 rule, 106–8, 173
Electronic Arts, 138
eMarketer.com, 212
entertainment, convergence of advertising with, 79, 80–84
entitlement, sense of, and consumer choice, 31–32
Entrepreneur, 2
entrepreneurial alliances. *See* partnerships
e-readers, 19–20, 112
Ericsson, 223
ESPN (Entertainment and Sports Programming Network), 29, 183
Etsy, 220–22
Exit41, 219–20
experts vs. amateurs, 47–51
extra cash, holding onto, 197–98

Facebook, 2, 51, 53, 55, 99, 105, 139–40
Facebook Ad Network, 120–21
"Facebook principle," 139–40
farmer's markets, 132–33
fax machines, 93
FedEx, 92
"fidelity swap," 154
Fielding, James, 156–57, 162
first factor. *See* consumer choice
First National Bank of Omaha, 104–5
fiscal prudence, 197–200
Flash-matic remote controls, 26
floating television spots, 101–2, 102–3
FM Sideband, 184
footwear, 125–27

Ford Fiesta, 187
four Cs (four factors), 6–14, 19–21.
    See also consumer choice; con-
    tent; convergence; curation
Fox, Megan, 97

Gahnz, Jeff J., 104
Gale, Porter, 208
garage-door openers, 25
gatekeepers, 93–97
Gates, Bill, 188
General Electric Theater (TV
    show), 80–81, 84–85
General Motors, 11
G.I. Joe, 136, 137
Gilder, George, 14–15
Gilt.com, 41–42
Gizmodo, 188–89
Godfrey, Nick, 121
Goldner, Brian, 136, 137
golf app, 130–32
Golf Digest, 173
Goodby, Berlin and Silverstein, 101
Good Guys, 154
Google, 44, 193
Google AdSense, 69, 86, 119
gourmet restaurants, 119–20
Granit, Yoram, 145–46, 149, 150,
    151, 158
Granjon, Jacques-Antoine, 175–76,
    189, 211
greenmarkets, 132–33
Greenwald, Julie, 170
gross earnings, 200
Groupon, 79–80

Hall, Taddy, 222–23
Harvard Business Publishing, 112,
    212–16

Hasbro, 135–38, 141, 191, 196, 224
hashtag, 98
HBO (Home Box Office), 29
Herbert, Don, 80
Hertzberg, Jesse, 220–21
He's Just Not That into You (movie),
    75
hiring, 196–97
Hollywood Reporter, 94
Home Depot, 72
Hub Magazine, 162
Huffington, Arianna, 50
Huffington Post (HuffPost),
    45–46, 50, 210
Hulbert Financial Digest, 180
Hulu, 16, 79, 88, 115–17, 191, 192

Ignatius, Adi, 212–13
iMovie, 28
information overload, 45–46
information scarcity, 9, 43–44, 45
Inman, Bradley, 186, 193
Invisible Hand, 154–55
iPad, 19, 159, 161
iPhone, 98, 99, 112, 113, 159, 223
iPod, 39, 159, 160
iTunes, 31, 39, 159–61, 170

Jackson, David, 86, 87, 198
Jarvis, Jeff, 200
J. Crew, 156, 162
JetBlue Airlines, 110, 172–73
Jobs, Steve, 161
Johnson & Johnson, 179, 211–12

Kallman, Craig, 170
Kendall, Tim, 120
Kilar, Jason, 16, 116, 191, 192
Kindle, 19, 112

Kinsley, Michael, 35
Kryptonite, 41, 98

Ladd, Alan, 80
Lagani, Dan, 19, 20
Lala, 31
Late Night with David Letterman
    (TV show), 28–29
laziness, and consumer choice,
    25–26, 30, 78
Lazy Bone remote controls, 26
legacy assets, 199–200
Lego, 63
libraries, 24–25
LinkedIn, 51, 55
"live plus three" ratings, 77–78
London Fog, 82–83
Long Tail, The (Anderson), 33
loyalty, 30–33, 153–63
Lundgren, Terry J., 204–5

Macht, Josh, 213
Macintosh, 159
Macy's, 140–41, 204–5
Mad Men (TV show), 82–83, 85
magazines, 5, 19–20, 74, 168,
    171–73, 178
Mailer, Norman, 61
Makinson, John, 150
Maney, Kevin, 154, 155
marketing, 69–90. *See also* viral
    marketing
  advertising as content, 86–88
  convergence of advertising with
    entertainment, 79, 80–84
  convergence of advertising with
    news and information, 79,
    84–86
  end of market segmentation,
    88–89

marketers fighting back, 73–75
new barriers to, 75–76
paying consumers for their
    attention, 79–80
purchase funnel, 71–73
as a relationship, 89–90
market segmentation, 88–89
MarketWatch, 180–81, 191–92,
    194–95
Marshall, Matt, 94–95
Martha Stewart Rule, 222–23
McDonald's, 154, 155
media convergence. *See* conver-
    gence
media experience, product as,
    125–34
Mediaite.com, 96
media layers, 132–34
Merchant of Venice (Shakespeare),
    43
microcurators, 95–96, 104
micro-payments, 42
Microsoft, 79
Million Penguins, A (wikinovel),
    150
Milton Bradley Company, 135
mindreading, 117–20
mistakes, acknowledgment of,
    97–99
Mobile Commons, 142, 223
Modelinia, 79
monetization. *See* revenue
Monseau, Marc, 211
Moonves, Leslie, 7
Morris, Sheila, 96, 99–100, 104
Morris Marketing and Entertain-
    ment, 96, 104
Movember, 108
movie trailers, 87
MP3 players, 31, 39, 170

Mr. Potato Head, 135
multimedia editors, 57–61
multiplier effect, 216–18
music downloads, 31–32, 170
My Little Pony, 135–36
MySpace, 51, 55, 99
"My Starbucks Idea," 142–43, 149
mystery novels, 60

Naf Naf, 176
National Do Not Call Registry, 76
National Public Radio, 60, 81
NBC (National Broadcast Company), 29, 37–38
NCAA Tournament, 201–4
Nespresso, 153, 157–58, 214–16
Netflix, 11
newness, 156–63
new newsroom, 207–24
    building entire businesses, 218–22
    change as only constant, 222–24
    evolving with the C-scape, 212–16
    multiplier effect, 216–18
    role of, 211–12
    two-way talk, 209–11
new privacy, 75–76
newspapers, 3–4, 11, 46, 114–15, 199. *See also specific newspapers*
    content and, 35–38, 41, 42
    convergence and, 57–59, 64–65, 79, 84–86
Newton, Isaac, 26
New York Times, 35–36, 40, 44, 46, 57, 72, 97, 162, 170, 179, 186
NFL Europe, 7
niches, 51

Nicolet National Bank, 104
Nielsen, 77–78
Nike, 144
Nikon, 223
Nintendo, 136, 137
Nokia, 223

optimism, 197
overhead, 154–55, 199
owned media, 216

paidcontent.org, 94
paid media, 216
Panasonic, 73
parallel distribution, 174
Paramount Pictures, 137
Parker Brothers, 135
Park Slope Courier, 102, 103
partnerships, 183–205
    approaches to, 192–94
    backing up risk-taking with fiscal prudence, 197–200
    bridging the gap between traditional and new cultures, 200–205
    convergent entrepreneurship, 194–97
    Datasport, 183–87
    everyone is your "consumer," 189–92
    Sarah Austin, 187–89
Pathfinder, 13
pay TV, 29
PCWorld.com, 99
Penguin Books, 150
Pepsico Amp, 98, 99
permission, new levels of, 75–76
Personal Branding, 187
personal computers (PCs), and productivity gains, 53–55

phone apps, 98–99, 111–13
  AccelGolf, 130–32
plane tickets, 128–30
Pogue, David, 72
Pokémon, 136
Politico, 94
"pre-roll" ads, 86–87, 88
presidential campaign of 2008,
    45–46, 50
"press relations" vs. "public rela-
    tions," 92
press releases, 93, 96
Pretty Woman (movie), 146–47
pricing, 168–69
  concierge, 171–77
  subscription model, 171–73,
    177–78
  traditional approaches to, 169–70
product
  as commodity, 153–56
  as media experience, 125–34
product design, 135–51
  co-creating, 144–45, 149–50
  company as experience curator,
    149–51
  concierge, 145–49
  experiences customers want,
    138–44
  pricing design and, 171–77
productivity, and technological
    innovations, 53–55
product placement, 79, 81, 82–84
professional experts vs. amateurs,
    47–51
public relations (PR), 91–108
  campaigning for long term,
    99–100
  80-20 rule, 106–8
  influence vs. control, 97–99

rise of convergent, 93–97
  viral marketing, 101–6
purchase funnel, 71–73

Quirky, 219
Quote.com, 11
QuoteTrek, 184

radio, 23–24, 38
railroad industry, 20, 192
Raj, Jon, 1–3, 224
Rayport, Jeffrey, 70–71, 118
Reader's Digest Media, 19
Reagan, Ronald, 80–81, 84–85
Redpoint Ventures, 69
remote controls, 25–27
revenue, 167–81. *See also* pricing
  backing up risk-taking with
    fiscal prudence, 197–200
  decline of traditional
    approaches, 169–70
  diversifying streams of, 180–81
  experimenting with business
    models, 41–42
  subscription model, 171–73,
    177–78
revenue sharing, 178–79
Rheingold, 106
Rice, Anne, 59
risk-taking, 193–94, 196–97
  backing up with fiscal prudence,
    197–200
Romanesko, Jim, 94
Rose, Charlie, 116, 191
Rosenschein, Bob, 69
Ross, John, 72

Saatchi & Saatchi, 92
sales data, 140–41

San Francisco Chronicle, 7, 101–4, 114–15, 199
San Francisco stadiums, 84
San Francisco 49ers, 7
San Jose Mercury News, 94
Sea of Shoes, 218–19
search engines, 37, 44, 79, 81–82
second factor. *See* content
Seeking Alpha, 86, 87, 198
Segway Personal Transporter, 5
Senk, Glen T., 218–19, 224
SFGate.com, 7, 9
Shakespeare, William, 43
Sharkey, Tina, 212
Shirky, Clay, 42
Silverman, Andrew, 120–21
skipping ads, 29–30, 73, 77–79
Sklar, Rachel, 96
Skurikhin, Andrey, 82–83
Slate, 35
Slattery, John, 82
smartphones, 30, 75–76, 111–12
social networking, 24, 45, 52, 139–40, 222–23
  customer service and, 115–17, 120–21
social overload, 52–55
Sopranos, The (TV show), 61
Southwest Airlines, 110
Space Command remote controls, 26–27
SPI Group, 82–83
sponsorships, 80–81
Sporting News, 185
Sportrax, 184–85, 193–94
Starbucks, 142–43, 149
Star Trek: New Voyages, 62
Stewart, Jimmy, 80
Stinchcomb, Matt, 221–22

stock market news, 180–81, 184
Stolichnaya, 82–83
storytelling technology, convergence in, 57–62
subscriptions, 8, 35–36, 39, 41, 42, 171–73, 177–78
"Subservient Chicken," 83–84, 104
Super Bowl, 33, 71, 92

TechCrunch, 93–94
telephones, 52–53
Terpin, Michael, 94
textbooks, 36–37, 150
third factor. *See* curation
Thompson, Robert, 62–63
time-shifted television, 29–30, 33
Time Warner, 12–14, 201
TiVo, 29–30, 39
Total Electricity Home, 80–81, 84–85
Trade-Off (Maney), 154, 155
traditional vs. new cultures, 200–205
Transformers (movies), 97, 136, 137
TV (television), 23–24, 36
  advertisements, 28, 29–30, 77–79, 101–2
  consumer shift from dependence to choice, 25–30
  DVRs, 29–30, 77–78, 141
  new convergences, 61–64
  ratings, 77–78
  remote controls, 25–27
  VCRs, 27–29, 31
TV Guide's Online Video Awards (2007), 62

Twitter, 51, 53, 55, 94, 97, 98, 116, 213
two-way talk, 209–11

University of Texas, 24
Urban Outfitters, 218–19, 224
USA Today, 57–59, 183
user-generated content, 145–51

"value traps," 198
Vanity Fair, 187
variety, 45–46
V CAST, 7
VCRs (video cassette recorders), 27–29, 31, 73, 141
Veneto Casino, 120–21
Vente-privee, 175–76, 189, 211
VentureBeat, 94–95
Veronis Suhler Stevenson (VSS), 70, 92
VHS (Video Home System), 27, 31
video rental stores, 28
viral marketing, 101–6
80-20 rule, 106–8
Virgin America, 208
Visa Business, 1–3
Visa Business Network (VBN), 2–3, 224
Vogue, 173, 190–91
Vook, 59, 186, 193

Walgreens, 79
Wall Street Journal, 2, 57, 94, 178–79, 188
Wanamaker, John, 70, 200
Washington Post, 35–36, 57, 58
Watch Mr. Wizard (TV show), 80
Weather.com, 112–13
Webvan, 199
Wendy's, 216–18
WhatIsFresh.com, 132–33
"wherever, however shopping," 111–12
WikiAnswers.com, 47–48, 49
Willard, Fred, 81–82, 92
Wolff, Michael, 161
Woot, 79–80
word of mouth, 96, 108, 111, 216
WordPress, 95
Wozniak, Steve, 188
WSJTravel, 178–79

Yahoo, 44
Yale University, 28
YouTube, 41, 47, 102

Zappos, 102–4, 126–27, 130
Zaslav, David, 138
Zenith Radio Corporation, 26
Zipcar, 31
Zucker, Jeff, 37–38